A Colourful Dose of Optimism

In the last year especially, we've become more familiar with the mantras extolling us to look after our well-being and to follow the science. Jules Standish combines both with a healthy dash of much-needed optimism and reminds us that we can all enhance our personal and professional lives by embracing the power of colour and positivity. Her *A Colourful Dose of Optimism* delivers exactly what it says on the tin. Just reading it lifts the spirits and opens our eyes to a spectrum of practical ideas to look good, feel good... and do good.

Iain Ferguson, Chairman, Red Ant Group

This is exactly what the doctor ordered!
A fabulous book, totally on point with the world as it is. Bringing so much positivity to our lives... something that has been lacking in recent times. I'm a 'Follower of Fashion' when it comes to Jules Standish... she is clever, witty and fun, and always thinks 'outside the box'. Her depth of knowledge using colour through mindfulness and holistic diagnosis is really quite astounding. Being a songwriter, I write lyrics using a similar process to Jules – stories with layers of colour, uplifting and positive vibes... "Sending You Love Across the World", creating calm, happiness and *A Colourful Dose of Optimism*!

Susie Webb, Singer/Songwriter of Bossa Nova albums

In Jules' exciting new book *A Colourful Dose of Optimism* she cleverly helps us identify happy colours for our wardrobes and our homes. With her positive outlook on life, Jules inspires us on how to use the power of colour to transform our lives and lift our spirits.

Karen Oppegard, Interior Consultant, Oppegard Designs

My world is about facilitating change in our thinking to enable change in the way we live our lives. The uniqueness of each of us is determined by so many different factors – too many to list here – but ultimately our goal is to find our genuine 'self' within by removing, through understanding, intrusive obstructions restricting our process. In *A Colourful Dose of Optimism* Jules offers a fascinating perspective through her exploration of the power of colour and the influence it can have on 'how' one is in the world.
Annie Hughes, Counsellor

Jules' favourite colour orange sums up her glorious self and her third magnificent book: warmth, joy, encouragement and positivity that will immediately flood into your life as soon as you start reading. *A Colourful Dose of Optimism* leads you to discovering a more vibrant and exciting way of exploring the world and looking after yourself and your home, for ultimate well-being, and to get you through whatever life may throw at you. Expertly written by Jules who not only lives and breathes her own happy colours but can help you find your colourful comfort zone too by following her simple and extremely effective steps to bring you and your home some very much needed joy and harmony.
Sian Clarke, Personal Stylist and colour tutor at the London College of Style

We all want to wear colour, yet our lack of knowledge and understanding has us hiding behind our dark blues and blacks, fearful of making an awkward mistake. If you are yearning to break out of your colour prison let Jules Standish help you match the right shades for your mood and feel the power of light.
Xan Phillips, Broadcaster and Creative Director

A Colourful Dose of Optimism

Prescribe your own Happy Colours to Feel Good NOW

A Colourful Dose of Optimism

Prescribe your own Happy Colours to Feel Good NOW

Jules Standish

BOOKS

Winchester, UK
Washington, USA

JOHN HUNT PUBLISHING

First published by O-Books, 2022
O-Books is an imprint of John Hunt Publishing Ltd., 3 East St., Alresford,
Hampshire SO24 9EE, UK
office@jhpbooks.com
www.johnhuntpublishing.com
www.o-books.com

For distributor details and how to order please visit the 'Ordering' section on our website.

Design: Stuart Davies

This book is not intended to be a substitute for professional medical (including mental health)
advice, diagnosis, or treatment. Always seek the advice of your physician or other qualified
health provider with any questions you may have regarding a medical condition.

UK: Printed and bound by CPI Group (UK) Ltd, Croydon, CR0 4YY
Printed in North America by CPI GPS partners

We operate a distinctive and ethical publishing philosophy in
all areas of our business, from our global network of authors to
production and worldwide distribution.

Contents

YOUR COLOUR PRESCRIPTION IMAGES
Once discovered, reveal and keep your Personal
Colour Prescription of happy colours with Seasonal
Images specifically created for readers of this book
at colourconsultancy.co.uk/my-colour-prescription/

Previous books

How Not to Wear Black
ISBN 978-1-84694-561-8

The *Essential Guide* to Mindful Dressing
ISBN 978-1-78535-492-2

Dedicated to my mum
Somewhere over the rainbow

Foreword

by **Wendy Elsmore, Director at the London College of Style**

Even as a young girl I instinctively understood the power of colour. I grew up in a family home filled with it, courtesy of my beautiful mum who had a natural affinity for mixing colour exquisitely to set the mood and atmosphere in each room. I remember the restful and positive mood in my 'blue room' painted by her in a delicate shade of sky against a striking navy and sunflower yellow wallpaper, and how that room filled me inwardly with peace and happiness. I can actually reawaken those feelings, even now.

For this and other reasons, *A Colourful Dose of Optimism* resonates deeply with me, as I'm sure it will with you too.

Knowing Jules professionally in her role as Head of Colour at the London College of Style, of which I am Director, and as a much-adored personal friend for many years, I am captivated by Jules' passion alongside her incredible skill to teach colour to all, and this book's potential to empower your life in a rainbow of colourful self-care.

For over two and half decades, I have worked as a Celebrity & Personal Stylist, and was formerly Resident Fashion Expert on ITV's *This Morning*. I've styled hundreds of women and men, as has Jules, and I've been privileged time and again to witness the powerful transformation that clothing and interior colours have on inner feelings and outer appearance.

Let *A Colourful Dose of Optimism* take you by the hand and lead you through a joyful riot of colourful exploration. This book is a whirlwind adventure and the ultimate colourful read, a solution to feeling great now, with Jules' colour magic literally helping you to "look on the bright side".

This book is also poignantly timed. At a time in human history when the world needs positivity, healing and joy, *A Colourful Dose of Optimism* shows you how to turn challenges into opportunities, whether dressing to work from home via Zoom, to win the job of your dreams, help deal with loss, looking to boost self-confidence or know how to work with colour to change the mood through your home. An incredible treat, the ultimate colourful guide for you and your home – I promise you may never look or 'feel' about colour in quite the same way again.

Acknowledgements

Writing this book amid a global pandemic, and with so many world changes occurring, has been a challenge, and it is my intention to hopefully bring everyone a colourful dose of optimism into their lives. As an independent colour consultant, I am always looking at ways to learn, do better and improve representation across my platform. I appreciate that whilst there are a number of influences on my work there are always more perspectives to consider which in part was why I was so keen to include the commentary of other thought leaders in the industry.

Whilst writing I do not intend to make any assumptions; I simply write from a place of passion for the work I do. I very much welcome your thoughts, as the reader, as to how my words and concepts apply to your specific circumstances. My intention is to have written a book which acts as a helpful resource to a great number of people from various backgrounds and with various outlooks, but I do not assume that I have got that balance right. Everything I do is used to help individuals feel more confident and happier, no matter race, age, sexuality or gender. My system of colour analysis aims to be a positive and different experience for every individual, and to be current in the world we live in today.

This book would not have been possible without having strong teams around me. So huge thanks to my loving and supportive family, Miles, Becca, Alex and Justin, and to all my wonderful, loyal friends, and Lucy Wheeler for her invaluable advice. Special appreciation goes to Lou, Charlotte, Rachel, Tracy, Fee, and a colourful shout out to Charlie, one of the most optimistic people I know. A big colourful dose of gratitude to those who have endorsed the book: Susie, Xan, Karen, Annie, Sian and Iain.

Thanks also to all the experts who have so generously contributed their 'top colour tips'. Whilst I have endeavoured to highlight many of the stylists, businesses and fashion brands I have had the privilege of training and working with, it has not been possible to put every single one in this book. However, my intention is for us all on a global platform to share the positive power of colour, even in some small way. It has been and continues to be a pleasure to join together with like-minded individuals who enjoy inspiring others with their colour work.

Special appreciation goes to Wendy Elsmore, the inspirational Director of the London College of Style, for agreeing to write the foreword of this book. I feel lucky to call her a dear friend, as well as having huge admiration for her talent as a stylist, and for heading up one of the leading educational platforms for students of fashion and style globally. It is no coincidence that a lot of the personal stylists mentioned in this book are LCS trained.

Finally, my great thanks to John Hunt Publishing for working with me on this colourful journey, sharing some light through the power of words and helping everyone tap into *A Colourful Dose of Optimism*.

Introduction

Look on the Bright Side

Whenever I think of the Monty Python song, *Always Look on the Bright Side of Life* and its whistling tune, it makes me smile, however sad or down I feel. Just hearing the chorus in my mind can have a positive effect on my mood. I also know that wearing my favourite colour (orange) has a similar effect. Having control over our own emotions and helping ourselves to feel upbeat and cheerful isn't always easy. I am sure you will agree though, it is empowering to know we can make ourselves feel better and not rely on others to do this for us.

I am not suggesting we all 'pretend' to be positive permanently, or not to be genuine about how we are feeling. However, when we live in times of anxiety and uncertainty, why not take control of the things you can change in a positive way. If you could write yourself a prescription today, would it be for instant happiness, optimism and hope?

Our lives have shifted and the world looks different. As a result, we are desperately seeking new ways to feel positive and hopeful, whilst also looking for potential solutions to many of the problems we face. The answer could lie very close to home. Through a holistic colour diagnostic system, I will provide you with the 'Perfect Plan' for simple, effective, transformative changes in your wardrobe and home. Backed up with some science and colour psychology, I will show you how to consider turning fearful, challenging situations into opportunities to feel happier and more confident, whilst looking good and staying in control of your emotions.

Just think for a moment, how do you feel when you see that first yellow daffodil of Spring after a long, dark Winter? An instant surge of joy with a big smile, because the 'hit of happiness' experienced can be influenced by the powerful impact that colours have on us, physically, emotionally and psychologically. Science suggests that smiling, whether real or forced, makes the brain release 'happy' hormones. So why not find colourful ways to smile throughout your day in order to keep experiencing and sharing joyful moments?

Colour is light, which we see visually as wavelengths that can have a direct effect on our body temperature and behaviour, albeit subconsciously a lot of the time. Certain colours at the hotter end of the spectrum, like passionate red, adventurous orange and joyful yellow, can be instantly stimulating to the senses. They help you feel uplifted, and encourage you to get busy, to exercise, or start something new or simply to be more positive and mentally active.

In contrast cooler colours can be experienced as calming, and wonderful stress busters in times of anxiety and fear. Shades of blue, green and purple, that are restful on the eyes, can actually help you feel more in control, to be more meditative and peaceful wherever you are.

As colour is so fundamental to our well-being my aim is to give you some tools to learn how to create balance in both your wardrobe and your home. Enjoy a sense of serenity and happiness through your colour choices, providing you with positive benefits in all areas of your life.

It's time to look on the bright side by boosting your mood and lifting your spirits in your home interiors and your closet. Give your wardrobe a raise, put the wow into your workwear, and rejoice in the comfort of casual dressing. Turn every room in your home into a harmonious and happy zone for yourself and your family. What everyone needs now is *A Colourful Dose of Optimism*, at work and at play.

How can this book help YOU?
Firstly, diagnose the problem
If you answer YES to one or more of the following questions,

then this book can help you.

Do you:

- look tired and drained and could do with a healthy, glowing appearance?
- struggle to find colours that flatter and suit you?
- need to get some energy to start a new project or exercise routine?
- feel stressed about a family situation & how to feel more in control?
- work from home and want to look your best on Zoom?
- have a job interview and are not sure what colours would be appropriate?
- have a wardrobe full of clothes you don't wear but hate shopping?
- would love to feel upbeat even in comfortable casuals?
- feel stressed about not having the time to invest in searching for outfits?
- want some inspiration to try new colour combinations but don't know how?
- consider it's time to have a more sustainable wardrobe?
- want to feel happier in your home as you can't afford to move?
- need to give your living area a new look to brighten it up, and have a tight budget?
- simply want to boost your outlook for a brighter future?

Your step-by-step guide to a positive prescription

Now you have diagnosed the problem(s), let's take a look at the possible solutions, and how we are going to get there:

Working with your 'Perfect Plan' for positive change is the *first step* to discovering your best colour palette that you genetically inherited, along with an exciting look at your individual characteristics. Analysing those inborn traits of introversion and extroversion, and what powerful personality combinations you may have will provide an in-depth look at your individual colours. I will then marry this with the psychological power of colour to highlight every layer of your being, ensuring that the real, authentic you can shine inside and out.

Once your colour diagnosis is complete, the *second step* is starting to prescribe your own colourful dose of optimism, in your wardrobe and the clothes you choose to wear, according to your own personal colour palette. Lift your mood in flattering colours that get you complimented, make you feel confident, with a healthy glowing complexion and youthful appearance. Put your personality on display and show your colourful side by discovering your key wardrobe colours, along with neutrals, accessories, jewellery, and make-up. Start to feel more comfortable and happier in your chosen colours, and never stand out for the wrong reasons or feel invisible again.

The *third step* will be taking you through an easy-to-follow detox and rebuild strategy. Get clarity and make more space, then create a seasonal colour capsule wardrobe of flattering items that will give you an instant hit of joy and happiness, every day. Discover how to look tonal trendy or classically clashing, go off-piste with colourful pairings, and feel positive in patterns or smiling in stripes!

I will show you how to enhance your body shape and energise your wardrobe with new colour combinations. Then learn how to shop effectively either online or in person, buying wisely for the new you. Knowing your happy colours can be a wonderful investment in your well-being for the future and help kick-start your wardrobe into a more sustainable zone. Your revitalized colourful wardrobe can then be positively focussed on the most important areas of your life at work and at home.

Step four is how to prescribe your own colour confident

'seasonal' work wardrobe and express your best authentic image in the office. When individuality is an advantage, combining colours can be a clever and empowering way to dress.

Discover 'top colour tips' to be camera ready, and embrace the new way to work from home virtually. If you are going to a job interview then stand out for the right reasons and dress appropriately for your profession, in your seasonal palette, to ensure that the impact you make in the first ten seconds gets you the job!

Step five is about how to be confidently cool in laidback loungewear wearing colourful casuals, a modern way to dress at leisure. The comfortable clothing market is big business with the rise of athleisure wear, luxe co-ords, joggers, jumpsuits, even smart pyjamas (yes, it's a 'thing'). My mission is to help keep you calm and relaxed in your cosy moments whilst staying out of the grey zone. Discover what colours are best for starting a new exercise or hobby, going on a date or playing games with your children.

Finally, you can prescribe yourself '*A Colourful Dose of Optimism*' in your home. By taking your individual palette and personality into your living environment you can create harmony and balance, surrounding yourself in colours that make you happy. Use colours mindfully in every room to elevate the space. Perhaps choose calming blues and greens to sleep in, but energise living areas with warming, stimulating yellows and reds. Add mood-boosting colour within a budget, without major renovation, and change rooms instantly.

To add to the level of expertise in the book, I am excited to be able to include some exclusive 'top tips' from expert Stylists, Interior Designers, Fashion, Jewellery and Accessory brands, worldwide. Those who specialise in helping people transform their wardrobes and homes by adding colour in exciting ways in their professional work and who will now share their amazing insights with you!

How I am qualified to help you; my colour story

I was eleven when my mum bought me a pink trouser suit. It was that sweet, bubble-gum pink, and when I look back, she was clearly ahead of her time, having dressed me in a super trendy 'colour block' outfit! I remember my friends being SO envious of that trouser suit; I even wore it with a matching headband – if only I knew just how 'in vogue' I was.

It was starting college, after years of going to school in a sombre, dark green uniform, that my real love of colour was given free rein. My wardrobe exploded into a kaleidoscope of bright yellow jeans, orange dungarees and purple satin jackets. All very 'happening' at the beginning of the 80s, as the era of punk gave way to the colourful fashion scene of the 'New Romantics'. As the lead singer in several bands myself, I fully indulged prancing around in this new fashion scene on stage!

Having worked in advertising and the travel industry, I gained along the way a diploma in Sales Promotion, Journalism, and Astrology. My interest in holistic well-being developed, particularly when I spent four years in the Far East. I have always loved to help people feel confident and happy, so having styled most of my friends, they encouraged me to qualify as a professional Colour Consultant and Personal Stylist.

I instantly fell in love with the transformational power of colour analysis and spent many years doing colour, styling, wardrobe edits, and personal shopping for clients. I was able to run my business with two small children which worked brilliantly for my lifestyle.

With years of expertise, I have adapted my own holistic system of working with colour, to create the Jules Standish Method. Delving deep into the wonderful world of psychology, whilst allowing the personality to shine through along with genetics, always ensuring that the skin takes centre stage. My work has been influenced by leading authorities in colour analysis. Namely founder member of the Federation of Image

Consultants Pat Scott-Vincent and the Colourflair system I trained in. As well as American Colourist Bernice Kentner, an advocate of seasonal colour analysis, whose book *Color Me a Season* helped encourage the 1980s boom in colour analysis.

Back in 2011 having worked with many people who loved to wear black but didn't suit it, I wrote my first book *How Not to Wear Black*. This went straight to number two in the Amazon 'Beauty & Fashion' listing. I had lots of fun with this book and still do. It really propelled me into the public arena of media and TV. I was featured in top magazines and newspapers worldwide. I appeared on ITV's *Breakfast Show* and a Sky chat show as a regular guest advising on colour and style. It was thrilling to be sharing the positive power of colour on such an elevated platform.

My second book *The Essential Guide to Mindful Dressing* was published in 2016. It highlights how colour psychology can be used positively through how we dress, along with the emotional support colours provide. The case studies in the book reflect how much I enjoyed working with people from all walks of life, experiencing how colours affected their moods and outlook in such beneficial ways. In business this knowledge can be key in projecting a positive image, whilst having a dramatic impact on others too.

However, my mum sadly died the week before the publication date. It was so hard to promote the book when I was devastated with such grief. I remember the radio interview I did at the time. I told the presenter I was wearing red to give myself a boost of energy, to project the passion I felt for colour, and to honour my mum whose favourite colour was red.

One of my greatest loves is teaching students of fashion and style how to incorporate colour into their work. For more than six years I have been a tutor at the London College of Style, educating, whilst sharing my colour knowledge. This is a real joy, especially knowing that many stylists are now helping people discover their true colours for ultimate well-being.

As one of the UK's leading colour specialists, my expertise and advice are often widely shared in books, magazines and in the press. Aside from my title as 'the Colour Counsellor' I am from time-to-time described as a Colour Expert and Colour Psychologist. Whilst I am a qualified Colour Consultant, I do not hold formal trainings in counselling or psychology but these are key areas of interest. With many years spent researching and implementing the psychology and science of colours, I find it fascinating to explore the hugely important role colours have in communication. I also believe that colours have the most incredible impact on how people look and are perceived, having a powerful influence on our surroundings too.

So here is my third book *A Colourful Dose of Optimism* bringing you over 16 years of expertise, combining all of my knowledge to help you create a joyful approach to living in harmony and happiness. Enjoy prescribing yourself some red to raise your glass to half full, pink for positivity, or yellow to put sunshine into a dull day. Or maybe choose blue for a calm outlook, along with balancing green to feel more in control.

Now, you can discover how to harness the power of colour to turn today's challenges into hope with a sunny outlook. Invest in yourself whilst enjoying the feel-good factor of having found your own colourful comfort zone for ultimate well-being.

Chapter 1

The Joy of Colour and its impact on you

Colours and culture – Seeing the light – Happy hormones

Colour, what does this word mean to you? Are you conscious of the millions of different colours that surround you every day, and how you can harness colour's beautiful rays in a positive way through what you wear and in your home?

Since time began, we have looked to colours and light for our survival. Whilst colours symbolise different things globally, they universally have a powerful impact on us all.

Life these days can be very demanding. The world is also facing huge challenges, which sometimes makes it hard to feel in control of what's happening around us. So gift yourself the ability to choose those colours that help lift you into a more positive and optimistic zone.

Create your own harmonious and balanced environment. Feel happy and contented, every day and for all events, whether staying in or venturing out. Discover how to project your true nature, selecting colours that create positive emotional responses, being psychologically supportive to you at home, at work and at play.

Colours and culture

In reality, there is no one-colour-fits-all as a fast solution to success. Colour symbolism varies globally. Prevailing colours are dependent on geographical and cultural preferences and have a direct effect on our individual experiences. However, we also need to consider the science, biology and our emotive reactions and feelings towards colours to gain the whole picture.

Whilst surrounded by colour everywhere in the world,

countries and cultures treat them all differently. Certain colours might represent a deep historical ritual or hold a traditional place within that specific region or belief system. I think respect should be shown as we cross cultures to adhere to age-old systems that ask us to be mindful of their requirements. If you have travelled to places either on holiday, for work or indeed have lived in a variety of countries, you will know how each one has its own memorable landscape, people, places and colours.

I was lucky enough to live in Hong Kong when I first got married, and wow was it a colourful place to be. I remember my first 24 hours having arrived at this incredibly energetic, buzzing metropolis and experiencing a complete assault on the senses. Chinese New Year celebrations were just beyond anything I had ever experienced. The memory of those bright, vibrant colours will stay with me forever and belong to a very happy part of my past.

Accepting that colours universally vary in significance and meaning, I have not gone into cultural details, but am keen to highlight this as an important part of being on our planet and living in harmony with others. So, let's celebrate colour together, and be inspired by the amazing benefits it brings, wherever we are in the world.

Tribe & Fable fashion & accessory brand founder Julia Watson's **top tip on embracing the worldwide language of colour:** *"For me colours are all about how they make you feel and the places and emotions they evoke. Think about colourful combinations like vibrant pink and orange often used together in India, the strong patterns and rich tones of Africa and the brightly blossomed prints from Japan. Then there are the feel-good calming colours of the oceans and nature. Colour changes our vibration and lifts us, transporting us virtually to other places."*

Seeing the light

When I do my colour presentations, I am aware that I might have some sceptics within the workplace. Those who wonder why and how colour can possibly make a difference to their image or how they feel. In the boardroom I am sometimes greeted with folded arms and blank faces, waiting for me to persuade them that wearing pink whilst being the height of fashion should be put into THEIR wardrobe!

So, the first thing I do is talk a bit about the background as to why colour can have such a powerful and positive influence on us. I am not a scientist and don't claim to be. It's important though to know the fundamentals of how colour can affect us on many levels, psychologically and physiologically. The degree it does will differ from one individual to the next, and of course we all have our own experiences with colour.

Colour has become part of our genetic code. Dating back to the early days of mankind when we relied upon a variety of colours experienced by the human eye in our natural habitat to aid in our survival. It's fascinating to realise that subconsciously our brains are reacting to colours all the time, day and night. It is the intuitive right side (female) that processes colour, whilst the intellectual left (masculine) side processes shape.

Nowadays, our sight is responsible for a lot of our experiences, and colours address a basic neurological and physical need for stimulation. Particularly as we live in a world where instant gratification is the norm, along with digital devices that constantly demand our attention.

Just consider SAD (Seasonal Affective Disorder), a modern-day condition that some people suffer from in the Winter, during short dark days and when light boxes can be beneficial to help boost people's mood. Light affects our internal clock which is finely tuned to activity and rest, directly linked to day and night. We all need a sufficient amount of light to regulate sleep patterns, whether young or old; the more balance we get the better our brains function along with our cognitive behaviour. So, we need light and colours around us for balance.

A few years ago, I was lucky enough to be asked to join Stephen Westland, Professor of Colour Science and Technology at the University of Leeds, to talk on the Radio 4 *Today* programme, discussing whether we all see colours differently. In fact, it sparked a Twitter debate, with followers passionately knocking back and forth the question of whether tennis balls are green or yellow.

Professor Westland is an expert on all things colour related, and he says, "Exposure to light in the morning, and blue/green light in particular, prompts the release of the hormone cortisol, which stimulates and wakes us up. In the late evening as the amount of light in sunlight is reduced, melatonin is released into the bloodstream and we become drowsy."

On blue's effects he goes further to explain: "There are multiple mechanisms for the effect of light on us. We know that bright blue light activates cells in the retina and can delay sleep. That is a physiological effect. On the other hand, the idea that blue is calming is a different mechanism; it's a psychological effect. So, in fact, it is possible for blue to be both calming and alerting. The calming effect is psychological and the alerting effect is physiological."

Calling upon my own research, here is a quick look at what I discovered on how our eyes play such an important part in seeing and processing colours around us:

- Colour is light and we see colour because of the way light is reflected off things or objects.
- Scientist Isaac Newton discovered in 1666 that all colours of the spectrum were contained in white light and when you shine light through a glass prism you get to see the rainbow.
- Albert Einstein early in the 1900s provided us with

information about spectral colours being made up of bundles of electromagnetic energy called photons and that these were more spaced out the longer the wavelength.

- Black is the absorption of light and white reflects light.
- The eye retina consists of photoreceptors that are tiny cells that respond to light, and these consist of rods and cones.
- We have three types of cones, which make us better at discerning colour than most mammals, but when it comes to colour vision, they beat us, as many birds and fish have four cone types, which means they see ultraviolet light which we can't.
- Back to photoreceptors; they transmit stimuli or signals to the visual centre of our eyes which translate into colours.
- Most of these stimuli we use for our sight and the rest stimulate our glands.
- Thus, light also affects in particular the hypothalamus in the brain along with the pituitary and the pineal, influencing hormones, heat, metabolism and our nervous system.
- Colours at the hotter end of the spectrum and longer wavelengths of light, red, orange and yellow can stimulate the senses, encouraging action, creating excitement and boosting energy.
- Colours at the cooler end of the spectrum, namely green, blue and violet/purple, have shorter wavelengths of light being more restful for our eyes with a soothing effect on the senses, sometimes reducing blood pressure and helping our nervous systems to keep calm.

Harness your happy hormones NOW

I think we all know that different glands in our body produce chemicals otherwise known as hormones. These hormones are an important part of bodily functions. Some of them can help to regulate mood, promote positivity and help us feel content. Sometimes, it's only possible to grab small, bite-sized morsels of joy or happiness. It would be unrealistic to assume that all of a sudden, you are singing from the rooftops with elation, but, even small changes can lift your spirits, and shift thinking.

Science suggests that smiling, whether fake or real, can encourage 'happy hormones' to be released because our brains take the smile as a trigger of joy. When you look at the smiling yellow emoji, you get the instant sunshine colour boost from yellow and the uplifting effect from the smile too. So, whether you really want to or not, smiling might be a great way to feel uplifted and raise the spirits of those you smile at too. Imagine therefore consciously choosing to wear and surround yourselves in colours that made you happy and smiling, how you could positively improve your mood in an instant.

Many activities and emotions can activate these hormones to react in different ways, so I thought it relevant to share with you what their purposes are and how they might just have a positive mood-boosting effect on you.

- **The feel-good hormone: dopamine** and the brain's neurotransmitter that is associated with pleasurable sensations which can be mood boosting.
- **The anxiety regulator: serotonin** – another hormone and neurotransmitter that can help you feel balanced. Once dopamine has been released, serotonin levels rise, affecting appetite, digestion, learning ability, and memory.
- **The love hormone: oxytocin** increases with physical affection, and once serotonin levels rise, oxytocin is produced and gives that lovely warm feeling of overall well-being and possibly also helps to decrease anxiety.
- **The pain reliever: endorphins** help you to feel positive and they kick in to support the body when in pain.

Endorphins increase with exercise, laughter, having fun and being intimate with someone. So, a hug isn't just a hug – it can be so much more beneficial than imagined!

Hug and smile – together! Those are my words of wisdom to end this section.

Colours' happy effects

Over the years I have written many articles for the media about the joy of wearing and seeing colours in our environment that might just be able to help us feel a little bit happier; to boost our moods and see things more positively. Here is some information you may find uplifting:

- **Light effects:** as discussed earlier in this chapter, our eyes visually absorb the rainbow of light and colours available to us throughout our daily lives. With the hotter colours having a stimulating effect on our senses and the cooler ones having a calming effect, via our hormonal system, namely the hypothalamus gland that governs heat and metabolism and affecting us all to varying degrees at any given time (and location).
- **Memories:** the brain is a remarkable thing, and as we all know has the ability to store away those joyful memories from the past. This might relate to a happy period in your life when certain colours are associated with those glorious moments. Subconsciously maybe you choose these colours over others because of the feel-good effect you experienced and continue to have whilst wearing them.
- **Reactions:** having a favourite colour, wearing it and getting complimented, with someone telling you how well you look in it or attractive, is enough to make you smile and say, "Hello, happy hormones!"

- **Rewiring:** when you wear the same colours that make you feel good over and over again maybe, with repetition, you could in effect teach yourself to be more optimistic.
- **Genetics:** your genetic colours determine which ones to wear that best harmonise with your skin tone and personality. Over the years I have come to appreciate what the famous Swiss Impressionist painter, Johannes Itten (1888-1967), noted in his work. When he observed his students' paintings, those with outgoing natures and warm skin tones tended to paint in golden/warm colours and those who were more introverted with cool skin tones used colder blue-based colours!

With my 'Perfect Plan' you can diagnose your own colours, and then prescribe yourself 'A Colourful Dose of Optimism'. Find those colours that make you feel joyful and upbeat and learn how to wear them in different ways. Alone, combined, for work, at leisure and in your own home, to feel a greater sense of control over your appearance and emotions. Now that's a positive reason to smile and release those happy hormones!

Frangipani "Shirts to live in" cofounder Benny Wilmot's top tip for colour happiness: "In the animal kingdom, the male is consistently more colourful than the female. The scientific reason for this is to attract a mate and therefore it seems reasonable to assume that you are more fanciable if you dress colourfully... in addition, I firmly believe that dressing colourfully, in a stylish manner, will make you happy. Especially when compared to wearing black or grey as these colours both zap and absorb energy."

Chapter 2

The 'Perfect Plan' for positive change

Your personal colour analysis diagnosed

Don't you just love a plan? I know that I do, because it's helpful to have a structure to work through when you might feel overwhelmed at the beginning of a new project. In this chapter, your 'Perfect Plan' is structured in three simple stages. Discover your genetic skin tone and individual colouring, followed by your most dominant character traits, then support your psychological needs at any given time. By the end of the chapter you will know which seasonal category you belong to. As well as those colours that totally align with your true authentic self, that have the power to make you feel happier and more joyful in all areas of your life.

Stage 1: Firstly, through colour analysis, discover how your genetics: skin tone, hair and eye colour can impact positively on your personal colouring. You can choose to look your most attractive, youthful and healthiest, giving yourself an instant 'facelift' wearing your best colours.

Stage 2: Secondly, you will begin your own colourful journey delving deep into your personality. This is a fascinating look at your true nature. Learn whether you have any dominant characteristics or a colourful combination of one or two, and how this can influence the way you express yourself and the colours you wear.

Stage 3: Finally, you are going to take a look at how colours can psychologically and emotionally help you be in a happier and more balanced zone, depending on what you need every day.

Stage 1: Treat yourself to a healthy and youthful complexion: your colour analysis diagnosed

There is no doubt in my mind that colour analysis works. Over the many years I have been a Professional Colour Consultant it always brings me much joy to see people having their 'light bulb' moment when they are introduced to their wow colours. It literally can be magical, and happens in an instant. The skin glows, the eyes sparkle, the hair looks lovely and everything becomes harmonious, and more often than not the client will SMILE. It's incredibly powerful and often transformational in many beneficial ways.

Colour analysis is to my mind a total feel-good treatment. The system that I use takes into account the whole person, not just the genetic, inherited skin tone which I base my colour draping accurately around, but a person's true nature. Why put someone who is predominantly shy, quiet and introverted in a bright orange outfit? Do they want to walk into a room and attract lots of attention? Probably not. It's about bringing the best out of each individual so they can shine inside and out in their own way, ultimately finding confidence being their authentic selves.

There have been many great influential people throughout the history of colour analysis, too many to go in to detail now. Of special note though is the famous Swiss artist Johannes Itten (1888-1967) of the Bauhaus School and his observations of the divisions of warm and cool colours. Also, the American Robert Dorr who founded the Color Key Corporation of America. Since 1941 his discoveries about colour harmony have been in constant use in clothing, cosmetics, paints, fabric and interior design.

Modern-day influencers of Colour Analysis include Carole Jackson and Suzanne Caygill. A great book with detailed instructions on skin tone, *Colour Me a Season* was published by the American cosmetologist Bernice Kentner in 1978. She put the skin as the central part of the analysis, accepting that eye and hair colour are important influences of the overall appearance. This ensured her clients always looked and felt their best, taking into consideration the relationships between colour harmonies and personality.

My method of colour analysis is influenced by Bernice Kentner's findings, as I also believe the complexion is the most vital focus of genetic analysis. Throughout a lifetime we often change our hair colour, so this might involve wearing colours in another seasonal category away from the face. It is my opinion that this point of difference should be acknowledged and is part of what makes the analysis individual to everyone.

Like Bernice, I also take a look at your inherited characteristics (more about this in Stage 2), and with this combined knowledge, I am able to prescribe you with your happy colours. Those that provide you with an effective, coordinating wardrobe with ease and harmony and that make you feel comfortable and contented for ultimate well-being in your home too.

Finding the colour palette that flatters you can be truly life-changing. However, I am also very much of the opinion that you should never be denied a colour that you love (wearing black!) if it makes you feel happy, confident or fashionable. It's all about how to wear it well away from your face so as not to harm your complexion.

First up in your 'Perfect Plan' is a fast, effective colour test requiring a 'Yes' or 'No' response to discovering your Warm or Cool seasonal palette. Secondly, self-analyse further by checking out the characteristics and differences between Warm, broken down into Spring and Autumn, and then Cool, Summer or Winter. Finally, take part in a quick, easy 'DIY' draping test, to help clarify your season even further, followed by my top 'Colour Discovery' tips as reinforcement and a checklist.

Award-winning podcaster Nancy Stevens' top tip for embracing colour analysis: "*Anyone can wear any colour, it's the shade, tone and tint that counts. You'll never regret wearing colour. People will respond in a positive way and it will put a SPRING in your step. One of the great revelations for me was that wearing the right colour means you don't have to wear much make-up.*"

Your PERFECT colours diagnosed

Are you 'Warm' or 'Cool'?

Four season analysis is inclusive of all ethnicities and is broken down into two warm seasons of Spring and Autumn whose skin tones have a golden-yellow at their foundation, and the cool Summer and Winter palettes who have blue-based skin tones. Within each particular season, however, there will be points of difference that determine which warm or cool palette suits you best.

- Do bright warm reds, greens and yellows look best? You are probably Spring.
- Do muted warm browns, orange and khaki look best? You are probably Autumn.
- Do cool pastel pinks, purple and blues look best? You are probably Summer.
- Do cool dynamic fuchsia, burgundy and black look best? You are probably Winter.

Your 'Colour Diagnostic' system starts NOW:

Four season colouring – which one are you?

Answer the following:

1. Do you tan a yellow/golden shade light or dark?
    If YES move directly on to warm skin tones.
2. Do you have freckles and/or burn in the sun and then go a golden tan, even if it's light?

If YES move directly on to warm skin tones.

3. Do you blush or flush when excited, embarrassed or had a drink (or two!)?
   If YES move directly on to warm skin tones (the Spring).

4. Do you have green eyes?
   If YES move directly on to warm skin tones.

5. Can you see green veins on the underside of your arm?
   If YES move directly on to warm skin tones.

6. Does gold look fabulous up against your face?
   If YES move directly on to warm skin tones.

7. Does wearing black up against your face (without make-up on!) make you look tired, panda-eyed, drained and/or older?
   If YES move directly on to warm skin tones.

If you answered NO to any of those, please look at these:

1. Is it really hard for you to tan, and if you do it's NOT golden?
   If YES please go to cool skin tones.

2. Can you see blue veins on the underside of your arm?
   If YES please go to cool skin tones.

3. Is your complexion either very light or very dark, without a high cheek colour?
   If YES please go to cool skin tones.

4. Is your complexion an overall pinkish shade but you don't blush?
   If YES please go to cool skin tones (the Summer).

5. Does wearing silver make your skin glow?
   If YES please go to cool skin tones.

6. Does wearing black make you look healthy and attractive, with an even skin tone and no signs of tiredness or ageing with dark shadows or lines?
   If YES please go to cool skin tones (the Winter).

WARM Seasons: yellow/golden undertones
Spring or Autumn?

Spring:

- A yellow/golden warm skin tone
- Tendency to blush/flush/a high cheek colour or broken veins
- Can tan a light golden to dark (redheads possibly won't)
- Complexion can range from light to very dark, can have an overall warm appearance
- Can have freckles
- Perhaps visible green veins on the underside of the arm
- Warm, yellow-based, bright and clear colours suit you best
- Hair can be light, mid or dark golden blonde, red, chestnut, auburn or sometimes black, but always with a golden glint
- Wearing black is NOT part of your colour palette, however, if you have black or very dark hair you could wear it away from your face
- Eyes can be clear blue, blue-green, green or brown

Autumn:

- A rich, golden warm skin tone
- Complexion can appear to have a bronze sheen to it
- Has the ability to tan a dark golden shade
- No high cheek colour (unless a medical issue) and no blushing
- Complexion can range from light to very dark, can have an overall warm appearance
- Can have freckles
- Perhaps visible green veins on the underside of the arm

- Muted, warm, golden-based earthy colours suit you best
- Hair can be dark blonde, auburn, chestnut, red, very dark brown or even sometimes black, but with a golden/red tint
- Wearing black is NOT part of your palette, however, if you have black or very dark hair you can wear it away from your face
- Eyes can be hazel, brown, green or more rarely blue

COOL Seasons: blue/pink undertones
Winter or Summer?

Winter:

- A cool skin tone with blue undertones
- No high cheek colouring (unless a medical issue) and no blushing effect
- Complexion can range from light to very dark, can have an overall cool appearance
- Generally, does not tan (definitely NOT a golden colour)
- Perhaps visible blue veins on the underside of the arm
- Strong, distinctive features
- Looks FABULOUS wearing black up against the face
- Best colours are vibrant, neon and cool
- Hair colour is generally either ash blonde, black, white or grey (with no golden warmth)
- Eyes can be cool violet blue or deep brown (rarely green)

Summer:

- A cool skin tone with blue undertones
- No high cheek colouring (unless a medical issue)
- Complexion can range from light to dark (rarely very dark)

- Can have an overall pinkish and cool look to the complexion
- Faint or light eyebrows
- Doesn't tan well (definitely NOT a golden colour)
- Perhaps visible blue veins on the underside of the arm
- Pastel shades in cool colours look lovely on you, best in pinks, blues and purples
- Hair colour is either ash blonde, grey, light or mid brown (with no gold)
- Wearing black is NOT part of your colour palette, however, if unusually you have black or very dark hair you can wear it away from your face
- Eyes can be blue (without yellow) or light brown

Your DIY home colour diagnostic test

This will help you discover your best warm/cool colours. Please follow these simple steps:

Prepare yourself:

- Sit/stand in front of a mirror to see yourself from the shoulders up
- Get as much natural light on your face as possible (if necessary, go outside)
- Keep glasses on if you need them to see yourself clearly
- Take off any make-up – lipstick colour in particular
- Tie back long hair

Colour test yourself:

- Put chosen colour item across your shoulders and UP AGAINST your face, no visible colours to be seen underneath
- Use lots of colours in different shades, including white

and cream
- Choose something bright and something muted
- Use cool silver and warm gold to determine a cool or warm skin tone
- Use pale cool pink or warm orange to also determine a cool or warm skin tone
- Use black to see if you have a cool, Winter skin tone
- Look carefully at your COMPLEXION first – this is very important

Your positive prescription colours will give you:

- An even complexion
- A healthy look
- A youthful appearance
- Glowing skin
- The WOW effect
- Sparkling eyes
- Less need for make-up if you wear it
- An overall harmony
- A smiling face

Colours that won't make you happy will give you one or more of the following:

- A tired look with dark shadows under the eye
- A washed-out and unhealthy appearance
- Red patches, or spots highlighted on the skin
- A double chin(s) imaginary or real
- Lines, wrinkles or distinctive signs of ageing
- Dark roots in your hair if it's dyed
- Looking like you need to put on concealer

Expert Stylist Elaine Davies's top tip on colour analysis: *"Get* *to know the colours that make you feel great by experimenting each day. Never discard a colour as not for you, just try different shades. Colour analysis will help you to find your fifty shades of best colours that really suit your personal skin tone."*

Top colour discovery tips:

- If BLACK looked fabulous up against your face (and be honest with yourself) and bright white and silver, then you are probably a cool Winter.
- GOLD will highlight a warm skin tone and SILVER a cool one. These two metallic shades will determine this important difference.
- If you have a high cheek colour or BLUSH, you are probably a Spring type.
- If you TAN a golden colour (light or dark) you are more likely to have a warm skin tone – Spring or Autumn.
- A colour should never stand out more than you do! When trying new ones on, blink and when you open your eyes, if you are overwhelmed by the colour then it's not right for you. If this doesn't work, imagine yourself walking into a room full of people and ask yourself, would they notice you first or the colour of your outfit?!
- Equally, you should never be 'invisible' in a colour so make sure you feel 'seen'.
- If in doubt wear BLUE! Oh yes this is the world's favourite colour, with a shade for everyone. Stick with a shade of turquoise if you are not sure of yours.

Stage 2: Put your positive personality on display: your colourful character diagnosed

Cheerful, adventurous, friendly, thoughtful, caring. Which characteristics would you say described you perfectly? In the boardroom, everyone's starting to chat now, wondering about their own personalities and how this might affect the colours they can wear. Keen to know what their true colours are to help climb the ladder of success in all areas of their lives.

I love sharing this part of the analysis, and how I have taken the teachings of many famous physicians and combined them with more modern approaches to create my own holistic way of diagnosis.

My belief, like many others, is that there is a strong connection between your genetically inherited colouring and basic characteristics that date back to the Greek Physician Hippocrates over 2,000 years ago.

When I first trained in Colour Analysis, this was a fascinating part of putting the puzzle together for every individual. But I won't lie, it's something I needed to prove to myself that had real value, to enhance people's discovery of their true colours. So, I did and found this method incredibly beneficial when diagnosing seasonal colour palettes. Over the years I have seen how positive it is for individuals to explore their characteristics and how this influences the colours they look and feel happiest and most confident in.

We all have positive and negative traits, and often a combination of characteristics that make us who we are. Taking this holistic approach means that you, as an individual, get to discover colours that you resonate with and love. Maybe your inherited skin tone is warm and belongs to the Spring seasonal palette. However, your personality is a mix of outgoing, sociable Spring along with a private, creative Summer side that needs to be acknowledged and nurtured. In this case, your personal palette may be best suited to the lighter, softer shades of bright, bold Spring.

Hippocrates had the view that a dominance of one seasonal characteristic could influence how a person looked and behaved. His theory being that the human body was made up of the four elements of air, water, fire and earth. That these correlated with four fluids known as 'Humours': the Sanguine which produced red blood from the heart; the Choleric which produced yellow bile from the liver; the Phlegmatic producing white phlegm from the lungs; and finally, the Melancholic which had black bile from the kidneys.

Many centuries later, the famous Greek physician and philosopher Claudius Galen took Hippocrates' theory further. He suggested that illness could be linked to imbalances in these bodily humours along with the fact that everyone belongs to one of the four named temperaments (see explanations of each below). His theory was upheld as influential for well over a thousand years. He set in motion a systemised method for the study of medicine, developed by others and valued by many.

After Galen, the four seasonal temperament types were developed further by the German philosophers Immanuel Kant (1724-1804) and Wilhelm Wundt (1832-1920). The latter known as one of the founders of modern psychology. Both contributed towards a deeper understanding that we now use in our modern world. With the expansion of the temperament traits, separating emotional characteristics and changeability in the types for clarity of differences.

In recent times, it was American Colour Theorist and Fashion Designer Suzanne Caygill (1911-1944) along with Colourist and Author Bernice Kentner (1929-2018) who matched harmony between personality types and inherited skin tones.

So, it's my pleasure to welcome you on this colourful journey of self-discovery. Seeing how these characteristics and correlating colours can have a positive psychological impact on your life is an exciting part of the analysis. Connecting your genetic skin tone colours, to your inherited character traits. Whilst we all are born inherently glass half full or empty, it's great to know that by taking control of those elements of your true nature and embracing your best colours, you can make your world a brighter place.

Which characteristics best relate to YOU?

Spring:

- Curious and interested in new things
- Finds exploration exciting
- Generally outgoing, extroverted, fun-loving
- Good at communicating
- Optimistic view on life
- Energetic and bubbly
- Sunny and youthful nature
- Likes to talk a lot, sometimes needs to breathe
- Enjoys the balance of being home along with being out and about
- Sociable, enjoys many friendships
- Can take on too many projects at once and feel frazzled
- Fails to always finish things once started
- Enjoys change

Autumn:

- Likes to be in charge of things
- Naturally outgoing, great fun at a social event
- A-Type workaholic, will keep going till a job is done
- Lots of energy, finds it hard to wind down
- Very disciplined and organised
- Good at delegating
- Dependable and reliable as a friend and work colleague
- Finishes the job once started, whatever the circumstances
- Determined and persevering
- Gets bored easily, needing new challenges to feel inspired
- Tendency to be tactless, but not meant to be, just being honest
- Driven to succeed

- Sometimes, can be domineering

Summer:

- Tactful, sensitive and loyal
- A wonderful diplomat
- Quietly spoken, sometimes difficult to be heard
- Likes working behind the scenes
- Enjoys 1-to-1 friendships rather than large groups
- Prefers staying in to going out and socialising in large crowds
- Generally, more introverted than extrovert
- Creative and practical, works at own pace to get things completed
- Patient, likes detailed work and handiwork
- Is a good listener but can get worn down with other people's problems
- Lacks energy to start new things, likes to work alone and not be pushed
- Not keen on change

Winter:

- A real stickler for perfection
- Does things to a high standard
- Sensitive, can be reactive to others' feelings
- Creative and often found working as a designer, artist or musician
- Generally, more introverted and enjoys having thinking time
- Very private and good at being in their own company
- Prefers to work alone, to allow the creative juices to flow uninterrupted
- Dependable and loyal once got to know

- A very analytical approach is taken to solving problems
- Elegant and dignified, always with their best face on
- Can be critical of themselves and others in their search for excellence

Find a happy balance

Hopefully you will recognise yourself in one of the above seasonal characters? Your 'Happy Colours' should be those that suit your inherited skin tone and also harmonise with your true nature. This is a powerful way to express who you are and can help you to feel centred and confident. Whilst there may be a dominant theme, it could be that you are strongly influenced by another season. For instance, if you recognise yourself as mainly Autumn but also feel some of the Spring characteristics belong to you, read about how your best colours will reflect a more vibrant, rich palette. It's important to wear colours that express your authentic self, whilst also projecting your best characteristics to help you achieve success in any area of your life.

I once worked with a public figure who was a Summer type, a true diplomat and quiet by nature. He had to make an important speech and requested my help to recommend colours to boost his confidence. My suggestion was a marine navy suit. A shade of blue for the cool Summer palette that showed strength of purpose and good communication, along with diplomacy, trust and reliability. I combined this with a purple tie, to inspire the crowd, along with a soft, pastel pink shirt, to highlight a compassionate nature.

It is possible that you may have shifted out of your true nature into something/someone else; do you recognise this in yourself? Some time ago, I helped a lovely lady who had suffered great loss and had a wardrobe almost entirely of black clothing. Her genetic skin tone was warm and Spring. Her character analysis had a high Spring score, but also showed a strong Winter influence. She had wrapped herself in dark clothing that didn't belong to her inherited colouring or personality, as she had hidden away, due to grief. This is perfectly natural and often necessary, to feel protected and keep your emotions hidden. She consulted me at a time when she felt ready to heal, and make positive changes through discovering her true colours. To begin with wearing small amounts of her Spring colours in the form of patterned scarves was all she could emotionally cope with. But it was a wonderful start on her journey to recovery.

Finally, it's important to point out that your culture and religion could also be a leading factor in the outcome of your scores, and of course the requirements for your dress code. Some people wear 'uniforms' which will not allow for their personalities to shine through their clothing. In these cases, I advise wearing coloured underwear!

Your CHARACTER combinations in detail

SPRING'S colour combos:

Spring with a hint of Autumn

You will be very outgoing, with a lot of energy and enthusiasm for life and new projects. Extrovert, and great fun at any social event. You will need to be mindful of your energy levels and try not to get overly stimulated and worn out. Take time for yourself to get into calm zones. Meditation, reading or anything that helps you unwind and relax will be wonderful. You really enjoy social events and going out with friends. It's important that you keep yourself busy with work, hobbies, exercising and having activities in the home.

Spring with a hint of Summer

Whilst you are a great communicator, your naturally more outgoing nature will be quieter and less active, with a Summer influence. You might be someone who shies away from the big crowds being more reserved. Preferring to work on your own and not always surrounded by others. Summer's natural diplomacy helps you think before you speak!

Spring with a hint of Winter

As a Spring you possibly have a love of wearing black. Many do! If you recognised some character traits from Winter then it could be you can wear black well. This is away from your face, along with other cool Winter colours too. It's important to allow both sides of your authentic self to shine through. Your naturally outgoing character can be beautifully balanced with Winter's need for privacy. Allow yourself time alone to work on creative projects; this colourful combination can be positive and productive.

AUTUMN'S colour combos:

Autumn with a hint of Spring

Wow, you are a live wire as this is a highly charged personality combination. You are more than likely very outgoing, extrovert and love a good party. With a powerful store of energy, drive and determination to get things done, you need to finish anything that you start. Your Spring influence tempers your high-speed lifestyle. It is beneficial to your health to slow down sometimes and find a relaxing hobby. This extrovert combination incorporates your fabulous organisational abilities along with Spring's communication skills. These highlight strengths in running a business.

Autumn with a hint of Summer

If this is you, then your extrovert nature will benefit from Summer's natural tendency to want to slow things down or create things away from the big social scene of life. With your outgoing personality and desire to achieve, this balance will allow you to stop and think before you act. Maybe consider a relaxing hobby rather than a high octane one. Summer brings some wonderfully diplomatic traits into your sometimes full-on approach and directness in communication.

Autumn with a hint of Winter

If this is you then let's consider how you combine the positive traits of the most extrovert personality with the most introvert. Your Winter influence brings both perfectionism and a strong analytic side to your natural drive, determination and leadership. This is indeed an incredibly dynamic duo. It allows you to concentrate on bringing your creative strengths into the business world for success in your field or in your personal life.

SUMMER'S colour combos:

Summer with a hint of Spring

You will probably be primarily a more introverted personality. Also you will have some of Spring's more outgoing traits that encourage you to get out and about more in your social life. With your wonderfully diplomatic nature, this influence might help you to feel more sociable and energetic. Ultimately enjoying being with larger groups of people, and taking risks.

Summer with a hint of Autumn

If this is your score then you will naturally be more introverted, but could enjoy running your own business away from the public arena. You will have the added drive and determination necessary to get things done in your own way and importantly in your own time. A lovely combination of Summer's creativity, along with Autumn's need to finish things.

Summer with a hint of Winter

You are no doubt hugely creative, a real perfectionist, super amazing with your hands, and probably make your own clothes, cushions, bookcases and pottery. My advice is to really indulge your creative talents whilst also concentrating on how best to enhance the analytical and appraising side of your personality. You have an incredible ability to spend lots of time alone to be really productive and create beautiful things.

WINTER'S colour combos:

Winter with a hint of Spring

If this is you then I am sure you can recognise your introverted nature, and whilst you need privacy and space, you probably get huge enjoyment using your creative abilities combined with an innate need to work with others. You are able to spend your time wisely, balancing being out and about, with being able to spend welcome time alone.

Winter with a hint of Autumn

Do you recognise yourself to be very introvert but also driven and determined to get things finished? You will be able to use your talent in creative abilities and turn this into a workable passion. Please consider combining your innate perfectionism with your mission to bring things to fruition. You can bring high energy to any art form.

Winter with a hint of Summer

With a quiet nature, you are probably someone who really enjoys spending time alone, either at home or in an environment where you are given lots of space. You have the wonderful ability to enjoy being alone. You find your own company of real benefit to you, allowing your creative talents to be fully explored. You are a very loyal and faithful friend. You probably have lots of people who want to lean on you or share their problems, due to your listening ear and diplomatic nature.

Stage 3: The feel-good psychology of colour: your colour therapy diagnosed

Colour psychology is currently popular, and if this subject is new to you, consider how influential colour is in the world of branding. How do you react when you see the Nike red logo? You probably recognise it as a product that might help you feel energised and run fast. Think then of the different response you might have to the high-end fashion label, Prada, which speaks of minimalism, elegance and understated leadership. So, for you personally, it's really important to understand how you FEEL about colours, your reactions to them and how they affect you. Your connection to colour needs to be conscious to really benefit positively from the rainbow available to you in your world.

Now, I am not a psychologist nor do I claim to be. I do, however, have a fascination with how colours psychologically affect us all. Having studied the subject, and researched it for all of my books, I personally enjoy the benefits of wearing certain colours to support myself emotionally. Plus, I draw on my experiences of working holistically using colour psychology with individuals from all walks of life. From stay-at-home parents to corporate clients, school leavers, TV personalities and Politicians, I have helped many people find balance and harmony in their lives through colour.

Other people's positive reactions to colours that we wear are also a big incentive to mindfully choose those that project a confident image. Nothing, however, is totally conclusive, and opinion varies on how much colour affects us. Maybe because of our culture, and the fact that we are all different, and react in our own individual way. It seems, however, there is little doubt that colour can expand our emotional feelings and connections to ourselves, to others and our environment.

I thought you might be interested to read about some important influencers in the world of colour psychology. Like the Swiss psychiatrist Carl Jung who in the early 1900s was considered one of the leading researchers of colour psychology, and created art therapies to help those suffering from trauma.

Some of the earliest applied colour research was undertaken by the psychologist Louis Cheskin at the Color Research Institute of America, founded in the 1930s. He was a pioneer in the field of marketing psychology, and discovered that we make automatic and non-conscious assessments based on colour along with other sensory factors. Red, for instance, is an evolutionary sign of dominance among the male animal kingdom.

Faber Birren had a highly successful colour consultancy business in American between the 1930s and 70s. He transformed many institutions with his colour work and put green firmly on the map as he felt that it was fresh, passive and calming. The colour green psychologically has been associated with personal growth, renewal, clear decision making and increased productivity. I love discovering new studies that have been carried out on the effects of colours in our everyday lives to influence us. Albeit so much of the time in a subconscious way.

A study was undertaken by lead researcher Dr Marlon Nieuwenhuis from the University of Twente, The Netherlands. She reported in her joint findings that "enriching a previously spartan space with plants served to increase productivity by 15%". How great for all of us to therefore incorporate some green in our working lives, or indeed any pastime that we love.

There is nothing new though in the way that the colour green has been used in hospitals for many years. It was back in 1914 that an American surgeon Dr Harry Sherman decided to turn his operating theatre entirely green. He found the glare of white lighting too bright and green complemented the red of the blood, helping his eyes to focus whilst operating. Green is after all the easiest colour to see, hence its association with balance and harmony. It is being used mindfully in branding these days to signify an 'eco-friendly' product.

Yellow on the other hand is one of the primary colours and known to be the hardest on our eyesight. It is mentally stimulating and affects the emotions and self-esteem; think of the instantaneous and joyous effect of seeing the first Spring daffodil or even a smiling emoji. When it comes to appetite using yellow plates can increase your food intake, whilst white will make the plate itself look bigger.

Let's take a closer look at the colour orange. Naturally stimulating and warm, it's interesting to know that the *International Journal of Research in Marketing* recently undertook a study in America. It suggested for certain charities using upsetting images against a warm, orange background actively encouraged people to part with up to three times more than their normal donations. They put this down to the fact that orange boosts the emotional impact it has on us, and as a warm, stimulating colour it makes us pay more attention.

Lots of experiments over the years have been undertaken with the colour red. Being at the hottest end of the colour spectrum, it is seen as the colour of passion, fire, danger, arousal, drive, ambition, and gives us energy. Red grabs attention fast and inspires confidence when used in marketing for make-up and fashion. Lipstick in red shades is a consistent best seller worldwide.

Professor Westland leads a research group at Leeds University where they have a "Lighting Laboratory" designed to evaluate the effect of light on human behaviour and psychology. Recent research found a small effect of coloured light on heart rate and blood pressure; red light raises it whilst blue light lowers it. A study from the University of Durham was carried out by Professors Russell Hill and Robert Barton from the Department of Anthropology. They discovered the participants who wore red at the 2004 Olympic games won up to 60% when competitors were closely matched (thus diminishing the obvious effect of ability). Professor Hill and Barton's team wrote, "In humans, red stimuli are perceived as more threatening and dominant than other colours, and wearing red increases the probability of winning sporting contests."

What is also fascinating about THIS research is that the team found:

> that clothing colour biases the perception of aggression, dominance and anger in strangers, outside of competitive or achievements contexts. This indicates that colour influences the categorical judgement of emotional expression and, specifically, that red hue is associated with a bias towards angry judgements... priming anger concepts (versus sadness) led participants to be more likely to perceive the colour red. Taken together, these findings suggest a clear association between the colour red and perceptions of anger, possibly related to the role of facial reddening as a natural signal of anger.

So, I think you get the colourful picture! There are lots of amazing studies happening all around the world on colour and I could go on, providing you with lots of data. But this book is all about YOU and how to harness the beneficial and positive effects that colour psychology can have for your ultimate well-being. Let's now take the next step and delve deeper to uncover new opportunities for your personal growth.

Mood-boosting favourites

This is where things get focussed in the boardroom. People are now leaning forward, listening intently and even smiling. Keen to understand how the positive psychological effects of colours can help THEM.

As you have seen, much research has been done to suggest

that colours can have a psychological impact on you. They can trigger neurological responses in your brain that in turn cause your glandular system to react, and produce feel-good hormones, vital to your well-being.

What is really interesting to you personally is to think about your own colour preferences which can be very emotive and often subconscious (aside from cultural influences). This could be down to the fact that rather than experiencing a rational response, you are reacting emotionally: maybe yellow brings back happy and fun memories as it was the colour of your playroom growing up.

Conversely you may have a colour that makes you turn green at the gills. Maybe you had to wear a shade of green as your school uniform and associate that period in your life as miserable or involving bad experiences. The physical benefits of wearing your favourite colours, can have immediate impact by lifting your moods and making you smile.

It's also important to note that every colour has a purpose, an influence and a power to alter your moods by stimulating or relaxing you. They can change the way you look and feel about yourself and how others view you. Blue is always popular in clothing, why? Not only is it the world's favourite, but also the colour most connected with good communication, trust and reliability. Whilst having the added benefit of being peaceful and soothing, just like looking at a beautiful blue sky and calming sea.

So, if you find yourself favouring a particular colour to wear because it makes you feel uplifted and happy, just think how powerful and intoxicating it could be if you chose a *combination* of colours that you love. How exciting to learn the psychological meaning of using them together, in a healthy, balanced and attractive way to highlight the best side of your personality, as well as looking fabulously chic and fashionable too. Of course bringing these combinations into your home is also a powerful way to lift your spirits and feel good.

Let's consider, for instance, putting trusty blue (reliable, loyal, great communication) with fiery red (passionate, energising, driven). Or impartial green (harmony, balance, strength) with magenta (fun-loving, compassionate). Then how about royal purple (inspirational, creative) with sunny yellow (joyful, optimistic, clarity of thought). An assault on your senses? Good, that's just a taster of what's available to you, which we will explore more of later.

Expert Stylist Kelly Hitchen's top tip for boosting your energy through colour: "When I'm feeling unwell or low on energy, my top tip is to look at what's needed and choose colour accordingly. A bright poppy red is a great colour to give me confidence and an emergency boost of energy if I have to speak at a public event. However, I find less stimulating colours like green will ground and balance me, giving me a more sustainable energy over a longer period of time. When it's time to rest, I choose a light soothing pink to comfort and relax me while my body restores itself."

Diagnose your own colour therapy

As we have already noted, you could be attracted to different colours for cultural or personal reasons. Your preferences may also change with your everyday needs. This could be at work, at leisure, or you may be drawn to specific colours to support you emotionally at different times in your life.

Sometimes people like to hide themselves in darker colours or ones that don't belong to their personal palette. This can happen during times of trauma, or when challenges shift us off our true path. This is perfectly normal and also necessary at certain times to feel safe, protected or hidden whilst dealing with emotional issues.

If this is you, then maybe adding some colour into your life in your best shades, to lift your mood and wrap you up in light and energy, can help get you back on track. See how putting black with red for instance can really raise the energy levels whilst still looking fashionable and smart.

So, think consciously about your needs in this moment, and have a read about colours and how to combine them. See if you can prescribe yourself a colourful dose of optimism right now!

How to wear the RAINBOW

Choose RED... for confidence and energy

Why: Red is the hottest colour so wear if you want to get noticed and stand out in a crowd – it's stimulating, energising and outgoing

When: If you feel the need to exert yourself, are tired or run-down

Starting a new exercise regime

On a first date to help get you in the mood

Going to an interview, inject some red into your outfit for confidence

Going for a work promotion to show you are driven and will get the job done

Sitting exams to keep you awake and alert

Making a speech, keeps everyone interested and shows you are passionate

With: Green, for a bold, dynamic look

Blue, to bring balance and calm to red's fiery nature

Pink, a great colour clash, with pink's compassionate side

Purple, a regal and dramatic pairing

Grey, for work, to represent good judgement

Black is striking, and brings authority to the mix

Brown, to ground red's passion

White/cream, allows red to shine

	Silver for cool skins and gold for warm, red creates evening drama
Shades:	Crimson, scarlet, garnet, vermillion, poppy, chilli, brick, raspberry, burgundy, true red, orange red
Positives:	Dynamic, passionate, driven, fiery, lively, noticeable, active, ambitious, outgoing, energising, romantic, strengthening, confidence boosting
Negatives:	Avoid if you are feeling particularly anxious, angry or have high blood pressure, and don't wear it if you don't want to get noticed

Expert Stylist Fleur McCrone's top tip for feeling good in red: "I love to exercise and the best colour to give me energy when working out is RED. This is because red is a dynamic and powerful colour that energises and gives strength. We often dress depending on our mood, and it's true that colour can change our mood too. Try putting on something really colourful next time you recognise that you are feeling a bit down and see for yourself the impact this can have on your day."

Choose ORANGE... for optimism and fun

Why:	Orange is the combination of energetic, fiery red and joyful optimistic yellow
	Frank Sinatra once famously said "orange is the happiest colour"
	It's great to wear to encourage feelings of hope and positivity
When:	To feel super confident at a social event with friends/family
	On a Zoom call to bring some fun and optimism to the party
	You need help to overcome an emotional trauma

To feel more adventurous and daring and step outside your comfort zone

Gaining some enthusiasm to get started on a new project or hobby

Generally, will encourage you to feel energised, positive and upbeat

At a family dinner, for some stimulating, fun chat

With: Blue, particularly turquoise, it's dynamic and full of fun and balancing

Pink, this colour clash will increase your energy

Brown is very stabilising and a warm friendly combo

Grey, as a professional pairing for work

Black is dynamic, but not a harmonious pairing, so do so with care

White/Cream, it's fresh, invigorating and allows orange to shine

Gold, it becomes luxurious, warm and beautiful

Shades: Peach, apricot, coral, terracotta, bright orange, burnt orange, tangerine

Positives: Sociable, happy, confident, optimistic, fun-loving, adventurous, daring, uplifting

Negatives: Avoid if you are feeling confused, anxious, hyperactive or have an upset stomach

Expert Stylist Sarah Cannon's top tip for wearing coral to feel good: "Colour really is power. One of my clients was asked if she'd lost weight when wearing a coral outfit for an evening event. This colour worn closest to her face made her skin glow and gave her the positive effect of looking slimmer and boosted her confidence."

Choose YELLOW… for mental stimulation and joy

Why: Yellow is associated with sunshine, warmth,

and joy

It affects our eyes the strongest, so its instant hit of happiness is linked to feelings of optimism, sunshine, self-esteem and creativity

Helps to make us smile, think of yellow emojis

When: If struggling with a lack of creativity, it stimulates the mind

Playing with children is a great way to encourage mental activity

If feeling low, it brings in the sunshine, with a smiley face

To help with clear thinking and decision making

If studying and taking exams to concentrate and get creative

To brighten up a dull day, anytime, anywhere

With: Purple, a dynamic, super creative and inspirational mix

Blue, always a popular combination, and very balancing emotionally

Grey is optimistic and joyful, putting the practicality into workwear

Brown, it makes yellow feel grounded, warm and approachable

Black is a dynamic combo, but beware the bumblebee effect

White/cream, shows clarity and professionalism

Gold, both bright and antique for a sophisticated look

Shades: Buttercup, primrose, bright, golden, pastel, lemon, canary, mustard, honey

Positives: Joyful, creative, sunny, uplifting, mentally stimulating, broadens the mind, clarifying and helps with decision making, increases self-esteem

Negatives: Avoid if you are feeling mentally overstimulated, frazzled or overly critical

Expert Stylist Sian Clarke's top tip for embracing the joy of yellow: "*Yellow is a striking and stimulating colour that champions clarity, intellect and most importantly, happiness. It evokes confidence so wear if you are having a wobbly day. Yellow brings some joy and sunshine into your world, and it's inspiring for others to see you wearing it too. I love putting yellow with blue, particularly at work, a combination that highlights trust, optimism and brings clarity and joy into the workplace.*"

Choose GREEN... for balance and productivity

Why: Green's wavelength of light is easy on the eye and calming just like being surrounded by nature's natural balance

              Wearing green clothing can help you to feel centred, creative and balanced

              Go green, it helps with clearing and detoxing, allowing space for new things

When: Wear it to work, or in your office to help increase creativity and productivity

              Starting a project or hobby, helps with new beginnings and a fresh outlook

              Moving forward in any area of your life; relationships; work

              If you feel run-down after an illness, give yourself a green strengthening tonic

              Needing to release anger and frustration to feel happier and freer

              For good decision making, choose green to be more objective

With: Red, for a bold, dynamic look that is very striking and uplifting

Pink, for a creative and happy hit of prosperity and friendliness

Blue is very harmonious, and peaceful

Grey, it becomes more sophisticated and office appropriate

Black, it smartens green up and is also businesslike for work

Brown, it becomes earthy and grounding, a comfortable combo

White/cream, lifts the emotions and is a lovely fresh look

Silver for cools and gold for warms, elevates green into a glamour scene

Shades:	Bottle, lime, forest, pine, bright, Kelly, mint, khaki, olive, emerald, jade, apple
Positives:	Balancing, harmonising, refreshing, renewing, humanitarian, friendly, sincere, creative
Negatives:	Avoid if you are feeling insecure or having trouble getting active or feeling super cautious about work or a project

Specialist jeweller Tarra Rosenbaum's top tip on the healing power of green stones: *"The beauty of green is how it hits the heart chakra. Bringing green into your jewellery can be wonderfully powerful, through the ancient technique of vitreous enamel as well as stones like malachite, peridot, or emerald. Peridot is one of the oldest stones and a little powerhouse of positivity. Emeralds will centre you with love and compassion while malachite will protect you from negative energy. Think of your jewellery as a talisman. As we walk through our journey in life, these are the things that empower us to be the best versions of our selves."*

Choose BLUE... for feeling calm and in control

Why: Blue has a short wavelength of light, so is easy on the eyes and restful

Probably a reason why it's famous for its calming ability in stressful times

It helps to keep us focussed for good concentration

It can reduce blood pressure and help with anxiety

Is often used as the dominant colour in medical centres and hospitals worldwide to help keep people feeling calm in a crisis

When: Feeling stressed or anxious, blue can help to keep your nerves under control

For job interviews, to encourage good communication and keep you composed

If starting a new venture, highlights a reliable and trusting nature

Giving a speech at work, or Zoom meetings, and need good diplomacy skills

Needing to feel trusted in any challenging situation

On a first date, will show you are trustworthy and to feel in control

Sitting exams, will help to keep you calm and aid with concentration

Through emotional traumas choose blue for a peaceful recovery

With: Orange, to stimulate blue's calmer nature and feel upbeat and positive

Peach, a soft version of orange, less stimulating than stronger shades

Pink is uplifting, and fun, a compassionate and caring combo

	Red, to fire up blue's cool side, for some energy and getting things done
	Black is always a fabulous choice, particularly for workwear, but try to keep out of the dark blue zone, turquoise or sky blue is a great choice
	White/cream is smart and add a bit of camel or beige with this combo, to tap into some Parisian chic! These add clarity and freshness to blue
	Silver for cools and gold for warms, adds sparkle to blue's conservatism
Shades:	Sky, cobalt, electric, bright, turquoise, aqua, pastel, navy, royal, teal, cornflower, cadet, denim, midnight, periwinkle
Positives:	Communicative, trustworthy, diplomatic, reliable, calming, dependable
Negatives:	Avoid if you are 'feeling blue' or withdrawn, particularly dark blue

Scarf Queen Jo Edwards' top tip for bringing blue into your world: "*Everyone loves to wear blue, men and women alike, and I incorporate blue into many of my scarves through patterns in lots of different shades to suit all skin tones and moods. It's such a lovely way to bring blue into your wardrobe in an easy and inexpensive way and will enhance any outfit.*"

Choose PINK... for kindness and support

Why:	Pink is the colour of love, romance, nurturing and compassion
	In its hotter shades is full of feisty fun and independence
	It's a youthful colour
When:	If you work in one of the caring professions or charities, this is a compassionate colour to wear
	If you are feeling friendly and want to have

some fun at a social event

With family at home, choose pink to share the love

Pink can help you get in touch with your own inner feelings

Can be a very empowering colour in its stronger, hotter shades

Shows a sensitive, caring nature in all situations

With: Blue, in particular turquoise, is a stunning combo and full of fun

Green, its balancing properties give pink some added strength

Purple, brings out your creative side, are cool and comfortable together

Grey, which makes pink practical especially at work

Black, gives pink a dynamic quality and a more authoritarian appeal, particularly in work environments, and gives it a grown-up look

White/cream, will reflect pink's fun and kindly nature

With silver for cool skin tones, and gold for warm, turns pink into a party zone

Shades: Fuchsia, flamingo, magenta, rose, carnation, salmon, coral, hot, mango, bubble-gum, barbie, pastel, strawberry, baby, plum

Positives: Nurturing, compassionate, caring, independent, sensitive, fun-loving, romantic

Negatives: Avoid pink if you are feeling particularly vulnerable or overly dependent on others for emotional support

Expert Stylist Nina Victoria's top tip on wearing pick-me-up pink: *"Pink is one of my favourite uplifting colours I advise you*

to wear. Whether it's a soft romantic shade that evokes notions of calmness and sensitivity, or vibrant hot bubble-gum pink that will help you feel youthful and full of fun. If you need some confidence, why not create a bold look and pair pink tones with luscious greens; the two complement each other beautifully and block colouring is a fabulous way to wear colour."

Choose PURPLE... for inspiration and meditation

Why: Violet has the shortest wavelength of light on the rainbow spectrum. This makes it the most restful of all colours

Purple is a mix of red and blue, so really envelops properties of both and its effects on you will depend what the ratio of these are

Purple encourages creativity and inspiration, is meditative and visionary

When: If you need to be the peacemaker at home, in family situations or get-togethers

At work, it is a great choice to help in all matters of mediation in a calming, unifying way

If you need to get those creative juices going, start painting that picture, or embark on a writing course

If you feel frazzled with life in general, start a meditation class or get yourself into a calm zone

Any form of yoga or Pilates, restorative and relaxing exercise routines will benefit from the calming qualities of purple

Delve deep into your spiritual side and get in touch with your subconscious needs and desires and discover a new way forward

With: Yellow will get you noticed, and bring some light cheeriness to purple's cool and more serious nature

Orange is a real head turner, and will raise confidence levels, taking purple into a more upbeat and sociable zone

Pink is a harmonious combo, full of compassion

With black to ramp up the creativity and for a truly striking look

Silver is a dramatic and dreamy combination and gold gives it a royal edge

Shades: Lavender, lilac, violet, ultraviolet, mulberry, mauve, deep purple

Positives: Inspiring, creative, meditative, peace-making, mediator

Negatives: Avoid if you are feeling very lonely

Expert Stylist Ania Bortnowska's top tip on feeling calm wearing purple: "*If you don't feel confident wearing head to toe purple, add accessories. I often wear my black coat which isn't my best colour with a purple set of gloves, scarf and hat in the colder months. This injection of beautiful purple helps to keep me calm and wearing a shade that flatters my skin tone is uplifting and makes me look healthy. In the Summer I opt for a bag and some purple shoes!*"

Choose BROWN... for security and grounding

Why: Brown relates to the earth, and the wonderful grounding and stabilising qualities that wearing this colour can bring

In times of distress and trauma, brown can offer comfort and is a super alternative to wearing black

When: It's a great neutral to add to other colours in your wardrobe

Is a naturally warming colour

Tones of brown in tan, caramel, chocolate can be worn beautifully together

	Add a bright pop of colour to make it look fabulous
With:	Orange for a rich, warming, friendly appearance
	Red to spice up brown's comfort zone
	Yellow, it brightens up a brown base
	Cream and white, it looks luxurious, chic and is a good balancer
	Gold, and bronze, either jewellery or metallic clothing, gives brown a real lift
	and elevates it on to the glamourous stage of eveningwear
	Silver cools it down and can provide an element of drama
Shades:	Caramel, camel, toffee, golden, chocolate, dark, beige, honey, chestnut, cocoa, taupe, tan, russet, buff, mocha
Positives:	Stable, secure, reliable, grounding, logical, dependable
Negatives:	Avoid if you feel uninspired or lack energy or enthusiasm

Entrepreneur founder of fashion brand Stoned & Waisted Rachel Allpress's top tip on how to look fabulously fashionable wearing brown: "Wrapping yourself in a beautiful shade of brown: tan, chocolate or honey tones looks great when paired with duck egg blue, pink, orange and also a neon bright. These offer surprisingly classic combinations and are often more flattering alternatives to wearing black."

Choose GREY... for good judgement and practicality

Why:	Grey is practical and all about fairness and staying in a neutral space
	Essentially grey is a combination of black and white, so a cool base, which can be warmed up

by adding some yellow to it

A softer, often more flattering alternative to wearing black

When: As a fabulous neutral shade, it's a popular colour to wear to work

It's practical, independent and a professional choice

Highlights fair judgement and the ability to be able to stay detached and take an objective view on things

Grey is a wonderful base in an outfit, that can be combined with your favourite colours to keep a good balance and allow others to shine

Please take care if choosing to wear an all-grey outfit, this can drain your energy if worn for long periods of time

Also, it won't do your complexion any favours either if it's in the wrong shade to suit you so wear it away from your face instead

With: Any of your favourite colours, as it will add a neutral base, bringing a practical and strengthening look to any outfit, highlighting other colours worn

Grey and silver look particularly appealing together, and this metallic really elevates grey into a glamorous world in the fashion stakes

Shades: Dove, charcoal, green-grey, gunmetal, slate, ash

Positives: Professional and dignified, shows good judgement, is calm and practical

Negatives: Avoid if you need some fun, get too serious or feel bogged down

Award nominated boutique owner Liz Trendle's top tip on toning down in grey: *"Grey is the perfect neutral colour to tone*

down bright vivid colours, such as coral and pink... and is much less harsh than wearing black."

Choose BLACK... for authority and mystery

Why: If you love to wear black you are not alone. I wrote my first book *How Not to Wear Black* back in 2011 to help people discover who could really wear it well and how to keep it in their wardrobe if it wasn't flattering

Black only truly suits the cool Winter skin tone and personality

If it's not in your seasonal palette, don't panic – continue to wear it but away from your face, for your complexion not to be affected detrimentally and combine with your best colours so as not to feel drained

When: Black means business, which is why it's so coveted in the corporate world

Black conveys mystery, is protective and keeps things hidden

In the evening, it's smart and chic and always 'in fashion'

Black loves to be authoritative and likes to lead, so wear it with care

If you are not a cool Winter type, please do be mindful about wearing too much black and for long periods of time

It isn't always flattering to wear up against your face, so choose a colourful scarf or jewellery to counteract the ageing, draining effects it can have

With: Cool pinks and reds for added confidence and fun

Most blues, a lovely mix of good communication,

and conservatism

Cool greens, makes this combination a harmonious balancing act

Purple is dreamy, and inspirational, a very creative combo

Silver for a hi-tech, sophisticated look, that is elegant and glitzy

Gold, warms it up and means that Springs and Autumns can find a happy way to wear it

Shades: Jet, ebony, onyx

Positives: Authoritative, strong-willed, projects control, likes to hide and be mysterious, chic, smart, protective

Negatives: Beware if it's not part of your seasonal palette, black can make even young complexions look tired so wear it away from your face

Fitness & Style expert Monica Huaza's top tip on harnessing black's power: "Like me, you can choose to wear black combined with a pop of bright colour like red, hot pink, royal blue or green. This allows me to establish my role as a leader while also being playful."

Choose WHITE & CREAM... for clarity and versatility

Why: These are lovely neutrals, especially in the warmer months

They represent clarity, and optimism, and create emotional space

Wearing white/cream allows other colours to shine

When: Brilliant and bright white belong to the cool, Winter season

Soft white is cool Summer

Off-white, ivory, yellow based is warm Spring/ Autumn

These reflect all other colours so allow them to take centre stage

They combine beautifully with all palettes, adding that crisp, clean look whenever you feel the need to wear it

An all-white/cream outfit can be very chic and fresh

Positives: White/cream are traditional, reassuring and simplistic, orderly, open-minded

Negatives: Avoid if you are feeling lonely, isolated or indecisive

Expert Stylist Liv Styler's top tip on how to wear white and feel good: "The beauty of white is that, whilst it does have a bad reputation in the practicality department, it can be worn with any other colour in your wardrobe, which instantly makes it super versatile. I prefer a white coat in the Winter to a black one (unless I'm walking the dogs!) as it's an instant mood lifter when worn with a bright coloured scarf!"

Choose GOLD... for glamour and glitz

Why: Gold is a warm colour, so suits all Spring and Autumn skin tones beautifully

It represents luxury

Choose gold as a celebratory colour, gift yourself a gold medal for success

Gold evokes glamour and is a fabulous evening option to wearing black

It is associated with magic and grandeur, wealth and riches

When: It looks chic and beautiful with Winter white or ivory

Particularly glamourous with shades of brown like caramel and toffee

Gold will brighten up any outfit day or night

It adds some fabulous sparkle and light to a black dress or jumpsuit

In jewellery gold will add some glitz to any outfit

As a metallic fashion statement gold can be worn as a jacket, top or dress with a chocolate stole for a special sparkly event or combine with a bright colour to really steal the show

Choose SILVER... for cool reflection

Why: Cool by nature, resourceful and imaginative

Silver is elegant and sophisticated

It's hi-tech and dreamy, and can be dressed up or down

There are no rules with this metallic, except keep it away from your face if you have a warm skin tone

On Summer and Winter complexions it looks divine

When: As a metallic, silver sits brightly alongside other cool shades

It looks dramatically fabulous with black

Appear uber cool and wear with icy pastels

Boost your mood with hot pink

Toughen it up with black, cobalt blue or ultraviolet for chic eveningwear

Combined with soft, cool shades silver shines its light in a delicate fashion

Silver is a precious metal in jewellery, that is associated with luxury

Assistant buyer at Kurt Geiger Daniel Shalom's top tip on the magic of metallics: "The great thing about metallics is the versatility they offer. Try pairing gold and silver with your denim and knitwear

or shimmer into evening with tailored outfits. A metallic can either be the singular statement piece to your look or can add another layer of texture. The wonderful thing is that you can choose your best metallic to match your skin tone."

Chapter 3

Discover your Happy Colours for ultimate well-being

Your personal colourful prescription
Spring – Autumn – Summer – Winter seasonal palettes
Key colours to wear up against your face and ideal neutrals
Your happy wardrobe colours; accessories; make-up; jewellery
Your best colours for personality combinations

What colour can do to BOOST you UP

- Put your personality on display and show your colourful side
- Get you complimented to feel confident
- Give you that 'wow you look well today' appearance
- Give you an instant facelift
- Highlight a glowing and healthy complexion
- Add a fashionable edge to a plain or neutral outfit
- Make you SMILE!
- Help you feel emotionally balanced and happy
- Give you a more sustainable wardrobe with your best colours
- Provide a wonderful investment for the future

Having followed me so far in this book, you will know I love to chat about how transformational colour can be once you discover your personal seasonal palette. Hopefully after following the 'Perfect Plan' you are basking in either your warm, Spring or Autumn colours or feeling cool in Summer or Winter. You will understand how your wonderful personality is all part of the holistic package.

You are now ready to take things one step further on your colourful journey, and become acquainted with your happy colours. You can then choose your favourites at any time, those that will support you emotionally, and help you feel more confident, at work and at play.

Each colour palette ties in beautifully with the seasons of nature we experience in the UK, and it can be incredibly helpful to visually imagine how each one relates to you and your best colours.

We begin with Spring's palette which is vibrant and bright just like the invigorating red tulips, yellow daffodils and new green shoots of this season. When we get to Summer, the landscape becomes faded due to the sun's light, so everything appears muted and paler, like the soft rosy pinks and lavender, with lovely blue skies.

Autumn arrives and the leaves turn golden, with burnt orange, olive green and rich earthy browns in the mix. Then comes Winter, with dramatic scenes of icy snow and crisp blue skies, and cool red berries on the holly trees. So, as you can see, each season has a 'look' and a 'feel' and those colours that also represent your season. Let's now explore this further.

SPRING'S colourful prescription in detail
Sunny, sociable, outgoing
Your 'Wow' colours are warm, bright and clear
You are the 'Communicator'

Spring's happy colouring

Complexion: Your complexion will range from either very fair (and possibly freckled) to very dark and can have a peaches and cream look to it (on paler Springs). With a yellow/golden warm skin undertone you will probably tan (unless very fair and/or redhead) a golden colour. One of the key things for you is the ability of your complexion to blush or flush when embarrassed, had a drink or through excitement. This might develop into broken veins as you age (NOT due to a medical condition). When you wear your Spring bright, warm colours these will beautifully harmonise with your complexion giving it a natural vibrant glow with a golden quality.

Eyes: It is likely you will have clear blue, blue-green, green or hazel/brown eyes.

Hair: You could be a natural redhead, have strawberry blonde or golden blonde hair, or very dark possibly even black hair. Remember that if you dye or highlight it, always keep to your 'golden' roots or you may damage the look of your fabulous golden-based complexion.

Spring's happy wardrobe

- Bright, warm, clear colours will be super flattering to your yellow/golden complexion and your sunny, outgoing nature.
- Your best shades will be the corals and peaches, yellow-golds, bright green, aqua turquoise, bright reds and oranges too.
- You may have a love of wearing black, and if you have been hiding in black consider shifting into your best neutrals of bright navy blue, warm-grey, tan and stone along with your brighter shades. Of course, keep black but wear it away from your face if you desire. However, be aware that it belongs to the cool palette of Winter and does not harmonise with your colouring so could damage the appearance of your complexion.
- If bright colours scare you initially, fair enough, start small and cheap. A T-shirt, polo shirt, a scarf or tie will do. See how you feel about your new bright shade and the flattering change it makes to your face and whether you get complimented. If you grow to love it, buy in quantity and splash out.

Key colours: *against your face*

- Red: bright, poppy, scarlet, pillar box, mango, bright red orange
- Orange: bright, mango, apricot, peach, coral
- Yellow: bright, daffodil, clear golden
- Green: bright, lime, bright emerald, blue-green, aqua
- Blue: bright, turquoise, periwinkle, light/bright navy, electric
- Pink: bright, hot, coral, salmon
- Purple: bright purple, bright violet, lilac
- Brown: camel, tan, golden brown, beige
- Cream: off-white, ivory
- Gold is your metallic

Key colours: *away from your face*

- Grey – light or dark the warmer the better
- Dark blue – marine or navy and bright
- Black works if you have black or very dark brown hair
- Khaki and/or chocolate brown works if you have auburn/ chestnut hair
- Avoid bright white

Ideal neutrals:

- Cream/ivory is your perfect neutral
- Camel and tan are excellent background colours to your brighter shades
- Stone
- Warm grey
- Bright navy

Your SPRING influences

Spring with a touch of Autumn:
Your colour palette may be really warm and vibrant too. The more stimulating reds, oranges and yellows being your preferred choices. Warm brown shades could also look fabulous incorporated into your wardrobe in the cooler months. Khaki green could be considered in the mix too.

Spring with a touch of Summer:
For you the really bright Spring colours might be too overwhelming. You could find yourself leaning towards the more pastel shades of the bright warm Spring palette. So, consider softer limes and delicate peaches, with blue and purple looking particularly lovely on you.

Spring with a touch of Winter:
Your colour palette could incorporate black away from your face, but probably navy blue will be best as your 'neutral'. Strong, dynamic jewel-like Spring shades, vibrant cobalt blues, purples, hot pinks and reds will suit you best.

Spring's happy accessories

- Shoes look good in tan, camel, grey and off-white
- Handbags and briefcases are best in warm tans, browns, blues and Spring colours
- Gold bags and/or gold shoes look great for eveningwear
- Ties with Spring colours combined with neutrals in patterns are work appropriate
- Scarves should be bright and vibrant, and worn to suit the occasion

Spring's happy jewellery

- Yellow gold metals
- Coloured gems to include turquoise, red and bright green
- Pearls provide a classic look

Spring's happy make-up

- Foundations are warm, yellow/gold based either light or dark to match your skin tone
- Blushers are peach based; peach-beige, peach-orange, apricot, coral, red-brown or golden-brown depending on your skin tone
- Eyeshadows are green and combos of green-gold, green-blue, gold and warm purple
- Eyeliners are green, gold, purple
- Mascara can be brown, green or black if you have dark hair
- Highlighter will be soft peach, cream, yellow-gold
- Lips are best in peach shades, apricot, coral, mango, and bright warm reds and pinks

Expert Stylist Laura Cruickshank's top tip on being a 'Spring': *"As a mother of 3 I rely on my amazing bright and vibrant Spring colours to give me energy. I use my outfits and accessories to give me a mood enhancing boost, and my purple hair helps to retain a sense of harmony; especially as my kids head towards their teenage years."*

AUTUMN'S colourful prescription in detail:
Driven, extrovert, leader
Your 'Wow' colours are warm, muted, earthy and rich
You are the 'Organiser'

Autumn's happy colouring

Complexion: Your skin will have a warm, yellow/golden undertone and can vary from light to very dark. The differences between you and Spring are that your complexion will have a richer and more metallic appearance. Also it won't have a noticeable high cheek colour or an ability to blush/flush (unless a medical condition or a Spring influence). Generally, you will tan a deep golden colour. You can wear a lot of make-up and unlike Spring look fabulous in rich browns. You will glow when you harmonise with your earthy, muted colours.

Eyes: Your eyes will be green, grey-green, hazel or brown, more rarely blue.

Hair: Your natural hair colour will be auburn, dark blonde, copper brown, chestnut or very dark brown with warm lights, sometimes black. When you colour your hair make sure you always keep the warm, golden/chestnut glow.

Autumn's happy wardrobe

- Warm, muted, earthy colours that recreate the richness of Autumn in nature will naturally lift your rich golden complexion
- Your best shades are those warm, glorious organic browns which combine beautifully with burnt orange, red-orange, olive and khaki green, teal blue, air force grey and rich purple (with some yellow behind it)
- Bronze and dark gold look fabulous worn as metallics
- These earthy tones that make you shine will be stabilising and grounding for you
- Pink is not one of your best colours, as your skin tone is golden based, but you shouldn't be deprived, so head towards muted pink, salmon or coral
- You are the only season who can rock wearing mustard yellow

- Wearing black is not in your colour range, so keep it away from your face

Key colours: *against your face*

- Red: orange-red, rust, brick, bittersweet, warm tomato red
- Orange: true orange, burnt orange, dark apricot, coral, mango, deep peach
- Yellow: mustard, golden, tan, camel
- Green: khaki, army, jade, moss, yellow-green, dark lime, olive
- Blue: teal, marine, muted turquoise
- Pink: dark salmon, dark peach, muted pink
- Purple: muted purple, warm deep purple
- Brown: chestnut, chocolate, coffee, bronze, camel, warm beige, caramel
- Cream: ivory, warm base with peach or coffee behind it
- Bronze and antique gold are your metals

Key colours: *away from your face*

- Grey – light or preferably dark, the warmer the better; military or charcoal grey
- Dark blue, warm marine or muted navy
- Black works only if you have black or very dark brown hair
- Avoid bright white

Ideal neutrals:

- Warm beige
- Camel and tan
- Honey

- Coffee-cream
- Chocolate brown

Your AUTUMN influences

Autumn with a dash of Spring:
Your rich Autumn colour palette will enjoy a more vibrant side, so if you feel you want to wear brighter shades of your muted colours, go for it. Emerald green, brighter yellows and lighter oranges, all on the hotter end of the colour wheel, will look fabulous combined with the peaches and creams you share.

Autumn with a dash of Summer:
In order to really benefit from both sides of your nature, you might feel more comfortable wearing the softer, pastel colours of your strong, rich Autumn palette. As you both share the muted shades, you can choose the sage greens, mauves, and marine blues.

Autumn with a dash of Winter:
You may well be an Autumn who is able to incorporate wearing black, along with your strong, warm palette of rich dark browns, and wear it well, away from your face. You will look fabulous and feel grounded when your wardrobe is full of rich, purposeful colours that suit your personality. Strong, dynamic forest green with true red will positively boost your mood.

Autumn's happy accessories

- Shoes look best in brown tones, followed by your other muted colours
- Handbags or briefcases in tan, chestnut or chocolate browns are great
- Black/white are not in your colour range so choose dark

brown or ivory/cream instead

- You can accessorise with either gold or bronze for an evening event
- Ties with your Autumn rich, earthy colours combined with neutrals in patterns are work appropriate
- Scarves should be warm, muted and rich, in block colours or patterns; leopard prints, Aztec, paisley and bold prints

Autumn's happy jewellery

- Bronze, copper and antique gold complement your skin tone
- Silver can be used if your hair is grey
- Your jewellery should have a bold, heavy chunkiness to it (unless you are very petite) with large stones in amber and dark green and big pearls or beads

Autumn's happy make-up

- Foundations are warm peach, and beige shades either light or dark
- Blushers are red-brown, golden-brown, true brown, rich apricot and coral
- Eyeshadows are warm browns, gold, khaki green, deep blue-greens or mauve
- Eyeliners are warm brown, khaki green or dark gold
- Mascara can be brown, green, purple or black if you have very dark features
- Highlighter will be gold, light beige or peach
- Lips are best in coral shades, brown, bronze, orange or deep warm reds

Expert Stylist Lynn Deards' top tip for wearing Autumn colours:
"Think of the shades of nature, those warm, rich, muted tones you see

on an autumnal walk in the woods, with the leaves creating a blanket of burnt orange, mustard yellows, khaki and olive greens, rust red, with mid browns and camel and wear them with joy."

SUMMER'S colourful prescription in detail:
Friendly, loyal, orderly
Your 'Wow' colours are cool, soft and pastel
You are the 'Diplomat'

Summer's happy colouring

Complexion: Your complexion has cool, blue undertones, generally light, or can sometimes be dark and you might be able to see blue veins on the underside of your arm. Your skin probably won't tan well/a golden colour. You do not blush or flush but might have an overall 'pink' appearance to your face.

When you wear your cool pastel shades in pinks, purples and blues your skin has a glow with a soft quality, which harmonises with your appearance. Black is not a colour that suits you, it is far too harsh for your colouring.

Eyes: Your eyes will be blue, or blue-grey, more rarely brown but not green (as these indicate a yellow-based undertone from the skin).

Hair: Your hair will be cool, either ash blonde, light to mid brown with no golden lights and rarely black.

Summer's happy wardrobe

- Soft, delicate and often pastel shades of blues, pinks and purples flatter your cool-based skin tone and complement your gentle nature
- Many of your Summer shades are softened by the addition of white
- Wearing black is not part of your palette even though you have a cool undertone, as it's too harsh for your colouring

- Coloured florals look lovely on you

Key colours: *against your face*

- Red: soft, pink-based reds like raspberry
- Orange: not really a cool colour, so not advised, but if desired then a soft pink-peach
- Yellow: pastel, soft and very light
- Green: delicate, mint and light grass green, pistachio, cool aqua, pastel blue-green
- Blue: one of Summer's best shades; baby, sky, light periwinkle, light navy, pale aqua, light turquoise, powder, blue-grey
- Pink: Summer excels in all soft pinks; rose, carnation, cherry blossom, watermelon, light magenta, baby pink, bubble-gum
- Purple: another one of Summer's favourites, lavender, mauve, light violet, plum, orchid
- Brown: cool taupe, almond, rose beige
- Off-white: nothing with a yellow base, but a pink pearl white is beautiful
- Silver is your metallic

Key colours: *away from your face*

- Navy blue, medium blue-grey, dark taupe, charcoal grey
- Rose beige, pale brown
- Off-white, silver grey
- Avoid bright white and black

Ideal neutrals:

- Soft white
- Taupe & almond

- Buff (pink base)
- Dove grey
- Soft navy blue

Your SUMMER influences

Summer with a tint of Spring:
Your colour palette could well be on the stronger, warmer side of the Summer palette which is predominantly cool and fairly pastel. The hotter pinks will give you added confidence, along with stronger blues and greens if needing to communicate in a group setting or at work.

Summer with a tint of Autumn:
Both of these colour palettes are muted, and this is helpful. So, your best colours will be those favourites of yours on the cool Summer side, with an added boost of heat. Such as raspberry reds for extra confidence, plus purple for feeling inspired and creative.

Summer with a tint of Winter:
Your preferred colours will be cool and icy with some vibrancy. With cool blues, pinks and purples, you may be able to wear stronger, darker shades of these, or black away from your face.

Summer's happy accessories

- Shoes in cool browns and all your cool colours are best
- Handbags and briefcases look good in cool browns, taupe, almond, beige
- Keep away from black, and instead use navy blue and grey
- Ties in pastel blues, pinks and purples are great and

combine well too

- Scarves in Summer pastel shades look fabulous against your face
- Patterns like florals will naturally suit you

Summer's happy jewellery

- Pearls, particularly pink ones
- Platinum, white or rose gold are your metals, along with silver
- Stones in pastel cool shades, like turquoise and rose quartz

Summer's happy make-up

- Foundations are cool, blue based with light rose shades best
- Blushers in soft rose pink shades
- Eyeshadows and liners are lavender, muted blues, greys, pink and silver for parties
- Mascara is lovely in soft shades of grey/brown and blue
- Highlighters in soft pinks and creams, with silver for evening
- Lips look best in cool muted pinks, raspberry, icy pastels

Expert Image Consultant Tracy Hooper's top tip for getting started with Summer colours: "When I work with a Summer, I always introduce them to their beautiful soft and delicate pastels first. Then I show them how to add in some of their stronger colours from their palette, like raspberry and deep lavender. These combined with Summer's neutrals of air force navy and dove grey, can look really fabulous when the whole look is put together."

WINTER'S colourful prescription in detail:
Trustworthy, perfectionist, creative
Your 'Wow' colours are cool, dramatic and strong
You are the 'Analyst'

Winter's happy colouring

Complexion: Your skin tone has blue undertones, and you may be able to see blue veins in the underside of your arm. Your complexion could range from light to very dark, and generally you don't tan well, and if you do it won't be golden. You do not have a high cheek colour or the ability to blush/flush (unless a medical condition or a Spring influence). Your features will be distinctive and as such you can wear a lot of strong, dramatic make-up without looking overdone. BLACK is your key colour and you wear it beautifully up against the face and brilliant white is brilliant on you!

Eyes: Your eyes will either be a deep violet blue, cool blue-grey, or very dark brown, not usually green (as these indicate a yellow-based undertone from the skin).

Hair: Your hair will be naturally either cool, ash blonde, platinum blonde, black or very dark brown, and white and grey hair looks amazing on you.

Winter's happy wardrobe

- Is all about minimalism and perfectionism
- Winter colours contain primary red, blue and yellow, and pure green, often darkened by the addition of black
- You have cool strong, magenta and fuchsia pinks in your palette
- The Monochrome look of brilliant white and black is amazing on you
- Keep your outfits always simple and dramatic, sometimes two colours are enough

- You suit the cool dynamic colours of black, white, electric blue, emerald green, burgundy, charcoal grey and silver
- Best colours are cool and strong, along with icy pastels in pinks and blue

Key colours: *up against your face and worn away*

- Red: blue red, true red, cool bright red, burgundy red, maroon
- Pink: fuchsia, magenta, plum, hot cool pink, icy pastel pink
- Blue: bright cool turquoise, cobalt, electric, icy pastel blue, dark navy
- Green: pine, emerald, dark jade, forest, pastel green
- Purple: blue-violet, royal, ultraviolet, deep purple
- Yellow: acid, neon, icy pastel yellow
- Grey: charcoal, grey-black, silver-grey, icy pastel grey
- Bright White
- Black

Ideal neutrals:

- Black
- Black-brown
- Navy blue
- Charcoal grey
- Brilliant white
- Pastel grey

Expert Stylist Tanya McMillan's top tip for positive dressing in black: "As a true Winter I absolutely love wearing those bold black pieces which I know add drama to my look and complement my features perfect. But, when I need a boost of positivity, I mix in a fabulous splash of fuchsia pink to inject some fun and energy to my *outfit. This instantly brightens up my mood, and in turn, my day."*

Your WINTER influences

Winter with a trace of Spring:
Your colours will be cool and probably lean towards the more vibrant, bright side of the Winter palette. With strong magentas and true reds being favourites, combined with black, charcoal grey and navy.

Winter with a trace of Autumn:
Your colours will be strong, and dynamic. Pastel shades probably won't make you feel that comfortable, because you need to express yourself in a powerful way. Think Winter brown, pine or forest green, and true red.

Winter with a trace of Summer:
Your colours will be icy cool, more on the softer, pastel colours of the Winter palette. With the blues, purples and pinks taking centre stage, along with black, dove grey and navy blue.

Winter's happy accessories

- Black, black, black!!! Shoes and bags can all be in black!
- Browns need to be very dark and best if match clothing
- White can be worn in the Summer, silver shoes and bags for the evening
- Winters don't need to make big statements with accessories, in your case less is more!
- Scarves and ties in patterns that are geometric, striped and anything dramatic

Winter's happy jewellery

- Platinum
- White gold
- Silver metal
- Diamonds
- Crystal and coloured gems of emeralds and rubies

Winter's happy make-up

- Foundations are cool, with blue undertones, whether you have light or dark skin
- Blushers in strong cool pinks and reds (avoid orange) will give your complexion a healthy look
- Eyeshadows in all cool blues will look lovely along with pink/purple in strong shades
- Eyeliner is either black or grey
- Mascara is best in black, and maybe grey as you age, blue can be a good party choice
- Highlighter can be either silver, grey or even pale pink
- Lips need a strong look, using blue-based pinks and cool reds

Expert Stylist Shanna Elizabeth's top tips on elevating your look with a colourful accessory for any season: "*Incorporating even just a smidgeon of colour into your outfit has the ability to not only elevate your look but can further boost your mood. One of my favourite subtle and inexpensive ways to do this is to select a bold earring in a colour which complements your skin tone. Because earrings are worn so close to your face, they can transform your complexion, allowing you to appear more youthful and radiant. You also have the added benefit of an extra colourful detail to personalise your outfit.*"

Chapter 4

Give your Wardrobe a raise

Make space, declutter, detox, shades of sustainability
Create a colour-coded capsule closet
Focus on your needs, budget & list
Joyful shopping, either in person or online

Shades of sustainability
Viable – supportive – balanced – justifiable – workable –
maintainable

ALL of these words are now achievable for your wardrobe, which can become more sustainable, efficient and joyful. You can begin to reap the benefits of enjoying a long-lasting relationship with the colours you love, and those that love you back. So, take the time now to give your wardrobe a thorough workout for a brighter future, which could be one of the best investments in yourself you could make.

Having discovered your colour palette, you may be super excited and want to go shopping straight away. However, please do take my advice and look at your current wardrobe and give it a makeover first. This approach can reap huge rewards for your wallet and give you a new level of sustainability by working with your individual seasonal colours first.

Maybe you already have some of your best colours in your wardrobe? Some pieces could be easily updated and revitalized by putting them together in fashionable new ways, colour combining or adding colourful accessories to items you love.

Having decluttered you can clearly structure a plan to purchase items based on what you need as priority and only in your correct colours. If your new palette is a big change, you will want to start by adding colours slowly and possibly on a budget, selecting key pieces that could make all the difference to your wardrobe. So, you can see why it's important to clear out your wardrobe first and then write down what you are missing, before you decide to shop.

When I qualified as a Professional Stylist and Colour Consultant, I used to love going to people's homes and doing wardrobe edits. It's amazing how many items one actually has that can be recreated in exciting and transformative ways. The changes could be as simple as buying a new colourful scarf to update some dark separates, or a patterned shirt that will go with neutral jackets.

Equally, clearing out clutter can be incredibly cathartic. Removing things that no longer serve you positively (or maybe never did!) is wonderfully liberating. It can help hit the refresh button for change in your life, shedding emotional and physical baggage to allow for new beginnings, only choosing colours that make you happy.

Everyone can benefit from getting the right colours into their wardrobes, and a few years ago I had the pleasure of revamping colours for television presenters. Being in the public eye means that wearing the wrong colour clothing can really detract from the message and end up as headlines instead of important news. Whilst their rails were impeccably put together with ease to source outfits, it was vitally important that only their best colours were available in their wardrobes to choose from, for appearing on screen.

You don't have to be on television to indulge in looking your best and feeling happy in your colours. There is every reason to benefit from a clutter-free, colourful wardrobe that serves to suit you and to benefit your lifestyle. Aside from the joy of getting complimented in your wow colours, it will save you time, energy, and a fortune not wasting money on things that don't get worn. You are also going some way to creating a more *sustainable* wardrobe for your future. So, let's get started on creating your happy 'colour capsule wardrobe'.

Feel-good in your new 'Colour Capsule' wardrobe

I am not one of those people that has the benefit of a huge walk-in wardrobe (I wish!); the rest of my family would argue my clothes take up most of the first floor, which is obviously not true! For me, each wardrobe holds items separated into those that are relevant to my everyday life and others for corporate work, special occasions and different seasonal requirements. So, I think I can relate to most of you when it comes to not being in a perfect wardrobe world, but let's join together in the joy of seeing what that could look like, and it's something to aspire towards, so here goes...

Neutral/colourful essentials:

1. Tees, polo shirts and vest tops: great for adding colour, layering and keeping warm
2. Shirts: super versatile in block or patterns
3. Knitwear: lightweight in Summer, chunky in Winter
4. Coats & Jackets: in your best colours for all weathers; a classic tailored coat in your neutral will last a lifetime
5. Jeans: the perfect pair to fit your shape in denim blue/black and/or white
6. Trousers: in your neutral shades or a colour in your palette
7. Skirts/dresses in block colours and prints
8. Suits: for work in neutrals or colours
9. Trainers/shoes
10. Gold or Silver jewellery (depending on colour season)

Personal pieces in your favourite colours:

1. Leather jacket

2. Trench coat
3. Loungewear/sweatshirts/tracksuits
4. Chinos/cotton/velvet/textured/patterned trousers
5. Leather trousers or skirts
6. Blouses/tops
7. A floral/patterned dress
8. Skirts: pleated, printed, rosy, tartan
9. Jumpsuits & camo trousers
10. Scarves & headbands
11. Ties
12. Pocket squares/handkerchiefs
13. Embellished collars
14. Coloured jewellery
15. Belts
16. Shoes & boots
17. Socks and tights
18. Bags

Now that you have an idea what to aim for, let's get started on how to achieve it, step by step.

Step 1: Make space

Clear, declutter, detox your wardrobe

It is my experience with clients that however much time and money is spent on clothes, very few people seem to be satisfied with what they have. I have heard the 'I've got nothing to wear' cry for help many times. However, clearing the way in your wardrobe to see only your best colours will make it a happy place to visit every day and can be life-changing, so, make this a fun experience. The purpose is to leave you with only those colours that make you truly joyful when you see and wear them. If they are missing, let's plan to purchase, slowly at first, in a structured way, taking your budget into consideration.

Your colourful action plan for clearing out:

- Aim to rearrange your wardrobe into 'best' and 'okay' colours, banning the baddies unless you love them to bits and they can be updated or refreshed with your colour palette.
- Give yourself time to do this and don't rush. It's important!
- Make sure you have some big bags to hand with labels and a pen. You will need to have different ones for: altering, recycling, reselling/swapping and giving to friends/family.
- Also invest in some storage bags and boxes with labels on.
- Please rehang everything on covered hangers, metal ones ruin nice clothes.
- You may want to put clothing into different colour categories.
- Be strategic, and start at one side of your wardrobe and pull out each item on a hanger. Then go through your drawers and/or cupboards in turn.

Ask these questions first for items that you get to keep:

Is it one of your best colours?

- It falls into your seasonal colour palette perfectly
- If it is not you can still wear it well 'away from your face'
- If it is not you can put a colourful accessory in your palette up against your face to counteract this
- It is a patterned item that has one or some of your best colours in it to camouflage its negative effect

Does it fit you well?

- The colour suits you, AND it is a good fit for your shape
- This item can be altered to make it fit well if you have changed shape
- You could add some a) shoulder pads, b) a belt to make it fit better

Is it a Classic?

- You wore it to an event a long time ago, but felt happy because it was flattering
- Even though you haven't worn it recently it will keep forever
- It was expensive and is in one of your best neutrals/ colours

If none of the above, put this item aside for charity, gifting, swapping or selling!

For those 'keepers' consider now: how much does your lifestyle NEED it?

I know this is a tricky one, because NEED and WANT are two words that mean different things and often the lines get blurred. Focus on whether your clothes fulfil your own personal lifestyle needs. To create a more sustainable wardrobe, colours need to belong to you, not your best friend or a favourite celebrity! Bring out the best of your authentic self, this is not about living someone else's life or style.

Each decade seems to return to fashion in some way, and 'Vintage' can be a key part to creating a sustainable closet too. If keeping older items that were flattering it's super exciting to create new stylish looks by combining them with more updated items or altering them. In today's world, we need to find ways to refresh our looks and wardrobes, whilst being as kind to the environment as possible, and choosing only your best colours will help you achieve this. The opportunities for change are endless and fun.

Look objectively at your NEEDS:

- Do you need lots of smart/formal wear if you work?
- Do you need some smart/casual colourful gear for going out?
- Do you need some classic outfits for event wear?
- Do you need some athletics wear for working out?
- Do you spend most of your time at home and need comfy clothing?
- Do you need new clothes because your body shape has changed?
- Do you consider each item's worth – think quality over quantity?

As a general rule, if you only wore this item/outfit once, is not a classic, was a bad sale purchase, has never got you complimented, is the wrong colour or no longer fits and can't be altered, then please consider giving it away to charity, or selling it. If you have a positive emotional attachment to it then ask yourself whether it's important to keep it for the memories and happiness it brings you.

Colourful conclusion:
You should now have your bags sorted into the following categories.

Bag one: Altering – repairing
Bag two: Recycling – charity
Bag three: Selling
Bag four: Giving away to friends – family

Everything that is the right colour and style, and appropriate for your lifestyle, should be back hanging in your wardrobe and in your drawers ready for colour coding. If it's looking a bit bare, don't panic; there is now room to fill your space only with those colours that will look truly fabulous!

Expert Stylist Terri Cooper's top tip on sorting colours in your wardrobe: "I advise my clients to start with small steps, to change the colours in their wardrobe. First, address your accessories, scarves, ties, lipsticks, earrings and necklaces as these are quick and simple ways to put colour into any outfit. Then move on to the rest of your wardrobe, seeing which colours flatter your face and make you feel good, embracing that positive shift."

Step 2: Create a colour-coded capsule closet

The aim:

- Get a hit of happiness and smile every time you open your wardrobe
- No more stress getting dressed
- Save time having your best colours & neutrals in order along with different combinations
- Give yourself lots of options in one space
- Ensure you have trans-seasonal pieces you can layer or change throughout the year
- See what's missing if you need to purchase something new for an event
- Add in a current fashion trend at a glance
- Save a fortune and don't buy things that don't get worn again
- Feel-good about starting out on a more sustainable path for a brighter future

Get into your neutral zone...

The following (and their warm or cool tints and shades) are basic neutrals:

Black – grey – navy – brown – white

Neutrals should be your clothing bezzies and form a solid foundation in your wardrobe, remaining there for many years to come. For this reason, they deserve some extra money and time spent on getting them right. Your neutrals play many important roles:

- They balance outfits
- They calm down bright or bold colours
- You might be having a neutral day
- An occasion might demand no colour
- They are safe
- They don't get noticed like colour does
- They tend to be classic items like coats/jackets
- You can have neutral bags, belts and shoes that give you a 'put together' look
- Wearing neutrals on your bottom half (trousers/jeans/ skirts) mean you can go all out with a colourful top or jacket

... and feel free to roam in your best colours:

Those that belong to your individual Colour Palette
Now you know your seasonal colours, you can add your favourites to your neutrals; the ones that make your skin glow, get you complimented and make you feel good too. Remember that there is a shade of every colour to suit everyone, to differing degrees, and this depends on your genetics, personality and your mood! It's entirely up to you how you now colour-code

your wardrobe; clash, combine or go classic for your lifestyle or personal preference.

Expert Stylist Vicky Wood's top tip on wearing neutrals with colour: "Don't languish in grey jumpers! Grey is a good neutral mixed with aqua and yellow and with red it's dynamic, looks delicate with pastels and comes alive with metallics. This versatile neutral elevates to another level once a colour is combined. Seeing my clients embracing new colours not only brings me great joy but it's a powerful reminder of how adding colour into a wardrobe can be such a life-changing experience for the better!"

COLOUR CREATIONS *can be so much fun and allow you to express your personality, experiment and play with your own colourful looks. See what can be made from current items you already own, or hopefully spark new ideas to update your wardrobe. Keep an open mind and see if any appeal to you...*

New colour combinations

Whatever your palette, check out your best colour combos from the previous chapter and see whether your new colours could be put together differently from your usual combinations.

Create the wow factor with them, by clashing, using tones, patterns, prints and benefit from the psychological effects of combining in your own individual way and begin your colourful journey of joy.

- Start with a pre-loved favourite item (or if you have rushed ahead and bought something new in one of your best colours then choose this).
- Try adding different coloured accessories: scarves, ties, jewellery, belts, socks, tights, bags or shoes to instantly brighten up an old friend.
- Take a jacket or suit, add on trousers, skirts, dresses

etc. which are not normally worn together in different colourways.

- Next, look to add different coloured shirts, tops and knitwear, in blocks or patterns.
- Look at buttons, are they worth renewing by adding some new colourful ones to brighten things up or metallic gold or silver for some high fashion shine?
- What about adding an embellished or colourful collar to an old crew neck jumper or jacket?
- Is it worth refreshing a favourite suit by buying it a completely new shirt?
- Putting a coloured coat over a neutral outfit can lift it into a rainbow zone.
- Check if you have a vintage item lurking that might have come back into fashion and can be combined in a current way with something you already own or plan to purchase.
- Authentic style can be created by putting old with new in your own individual colourful way so experiment and enjoy, you may happily surprise yourself.
- A pair of trendy trainers can instantly inject high fashion into an old trouser suit.

Top colour tips for looking TONAL trendy:

What it is:
Using one colour, take the shades, tones, tints and create one outfit (a shade is a colour with black added, a tone with grey, and a tint with white).

Why:
Tonal dressing is a clever and possibly new way for you to wear what you have. It can be stylish, slimming and simple to do. Here's how:

- Use your personal family of either COOL or WARM colours and mix shades, tones and tints together
- Team your pastels with darker shades
- Put your light shades with bright ones
- Textures and tailoring can be used to create your own authentic tonal look; do denim blue with a turquoise silk shirt and a navy leather jacket
- Put a pop of colour in an accessory to make this look your own

Look COOL or WARM things up in your TONAL palette:
Red & Pink in tonal togetherness with most pinks being a combo of red with white added, but when you put blue into the mix, becoming cooler. It's often a fashionable and stylish way to dress and slightly throws out the rule book:
Cool: Raspberry, rose, icy pink with watermelon red, true red, deep fuchsia, magenta or carnation
Warm: Mango, peachy-pink, muted soft pink with tomato red, bright red
Orange is for warm seasons mainly and is a combo of red and yellow:
Cool: Pale pink-peach with neon orange
Warm: Apricot, peach, salmon with coral, pumpkin, terracotta, burnt/bright orange
Yellow is far from mellow and not a favourite for cool complexions but it can work:
Cool: Lemon yellow, icy and pastel yellow, with neon yellow
Warm: Go nuts! Butter, light bright yellow, ivory with mustard, bright yellow, tan, golden, bronze, daffodil
Green is a walk in the park as it can go cooler or warmer depending on the mix:
Cool: Mint, grey-green, pastel and icy shades with forest, pine and deep emerald
Warm: Sage, moss, apple, pale lime with khaki, olive, dark

jade and bright green

Blue is a winner for everyone particularly cool combos:

Cool: Cornflower, powder, sky, icy pastel with dark navy, cobalt, electric

Warm: Aqua, light turquoise with bright navy, marine blue and teal

Purple has a lot of cool blue in it but warms up with red:

Cool: Lavender, mauve, light violet, with ultraviolet, deep purple and aubergine

Warm: Lilac, muted purple with bright purple or deep muted purple

Brown either has a natural yellow base or more of a pink one:

Cool: Taupe, almond, rose beige with black-brown, dark chocolate, cocoa

Warm: Coffee-cream, ecru, honey with toffee, caramel, chestnut, mocha, tan

Black & Grey sit happily side by side in the cool camp! Add some yellow and it warms things up a tad:

Cool: Soft blue-grey, dove, icy grey with charcoal or jet black

Warm: Light green-grey with dark green-grey (wear black or charcoal grey away from your face)

White & Cream are the dream team either cool or warm:

Cool: Brilliant white, soft white with added pink or grey

Warm: Off-white, ivory, oyster, cream, ecru, coffee-cream, magnolia

COLOUR CLASHING for an eye-catching look:

What it is:

Generally, this is putting colours together that sit opposite each other on the colour wheel or anything that takes your fancy and projects your personality.

Also, warm and cool together often clash.

Why:

It's a bold, stand-out look that gets you noticed. It also combines colours psychologically that can help each other out, emotionally.

How:

Bold, block and often bright! Or be more subtle and cleverly combine in a pattern or print.

CLASSIC clashes:

If you stick to the colour wheel, they are red and green, blue and orange, yellow and purple.

Red & Green:

A combination of high energy red which gets calmed down by green's balancing act. Bright and bold is best, or go pastel for a soft Summer look.

Blue & Orange:

Orange's stimulating hues can be brought to balance by blue, and teaming turquoise shades with bright orange or peach is fab.

Yellow & Purple:

Joyful, sunny yellow is joined by inspirational, dreamy purples and violet. Bright and neon is a real knockout, or muted is a more conservative way to do it.

OFF-PISTE pairings:

Pink is the star of this show, loved by lots of you, high fashion and why not!

Pink & Green:

Compassionate, fun-loving perky pink gets a freshen up with bold greens, best in hot shades.

Pink & Orange:

This is one for the sunglasses! Pick me up pink with bright orange is not one to stay in the shade, but combines a really sociable, outgoing, adventurous appearance.

Pink & Red:
For these to clash they have to be bright or bold or both! Hot, fuchsia, mango pink combined with fiery true red is not for the faint-hearted, but a really romantic couple.

Pink & Purple:
Fun-loving, dreamy, inspiring with a hint of glamour and luxury.

Pink & Turquoise:
Pairing hot pink with turquoise is a fab duo for warmer months, and these vibrant shades of generally cooling colours definitely play off each other.

Expert Stylist Saasha Scaife's top tip for clever colour combining: "I particularly love a good colour combo, my favourite being pink and red. They complement each other so well. Look at the colours in your wardrobe, you would be amazed at the combinations you can put together you probably already own."

POSITIVE patterns & SMILING stripes:
The addition of patterns, prints along with stripes and geometrics can all have a happy place in your new wardrobe, along with bold, block colours. These are just some colourful ideas:

Leopard print: always a fashion favourite and no longer resigned to be black and brown! You can mix any of your colourful shades into this pattern, or stick with your palette and either go warm tan brown and chocolate or classic cool black and beige.

Camouflage: casual comfy dressing in a fashionable way.

Stripes: can be in any colour of your choice, not just classic nautical blue and white. An added reason to smile is they can elongate your body where you want to slim things down, or widen a narrow chest to balance your body. Perfect for more traditional ties.

Geometrics: allow lots of your favourite colours to be combined in a statement pattern.

Florals: are fun and fashionable, highlighting your romantic side, either in full bloom or ditzy daisy prints, in ties, scarves, dresses and shirts.

Ridley London founder & designer Camilla Ridley's top tip on the positive power of colourful print dresses: "*Colourful print introduces versatility into wardrobes, enabling us to experiment with bolder on-trend colours in a safer, more controlled way. For instance, transform yellow into a dainty floral print and place it on a navy-blue background and suddenly you have the basis of a garment that will flatter almost anyone. Dress it up with heels, wear it with a blazer for a more formal event or a pair of trainers and a denim jacket or boots and a biker for a more relaxed look. The more colours in the print, the more options available teaming it with different coloured accessories.*"

Colour tips to help balance your body shape:

- Wear stronger, brighter colours on your best body bits to make them more noticeable.
- Bright and light colours should run up and down the middle part of your body with darker ones on the outside for a flattering slimline look.
- Darker shades look best on badly proportioned or larger areas to make them appear less noticeable.
- Wear colours from the same harmonious family to balance out your body shape. So, if you belong to a warm season, stick to Spring or Autumn, and if you are cool, then Summer or Winter. That way colours will blend into each other, because the eye will glide easily over them.
- A one colour, block outfit worn with a patterned scarf

will detract away from any area you want to avoid highlighting and draw the eye up to the face.

Expert Stylist Abbey Booth's top tip on revamping your wardrobe with colour for your body shape: "Through my work with body shape confidence, I use colours and prints to enhance a client's body shape and elevate their look. If you are pear-shaped, I would suggest wearing brighter colours and prints on your top half and darker colours on the bottom half to balance your proportions and draw the eye upwards away from the hip area. Tucking in to emphasise a small waist also helps! People often don't realise the impact wearing the right colours has on creating balance in their body shape and the positive impact it has on those around them."

Storage & sustainability

Store your clothes well and they will reward you with longevity. It figures that if you can keep items away from the horrors of moths, dust and damp, by looking after them carefully, you can ensure your favourites stay with you over the years. Having allocated places in your home that keep your clothes in good shape, give them space and protection so you know they are being cared for as well as being super organised.

Dressers/drawers

Start with the top drawer and the smallest items you wear the most; underwear, socks, T-shirts in the top ones, and sweaters, long sleeves, sweatshirts at the lowest ones. Put favourite colours at the front of your drawers or on the top of a pile. Get some display boxes that fit into drawers and storage bags to put sweaters, thick scarves, hats and gloves away. Store anything that isn't going to get worn in the current season. In Spring it's good to get your Winter woollies out of sight to create space for your Summer things.

Wardrobes

If you are lucky enough to have a walk-in wardrobe, then you will probably have space to house all seasonal wear together. If not then you need to be more creative and hopefully have a cupboard to put your coats in separately. However many wardrobes you have or have not, here are some of my colourful suggestions on how to arrange each one to suit your lifestyle.

Your Wardrobe by colour:

- FOLLOW THE RAINBOW:
  Use the rainbow structure and start either on the left or right of each wardrobe in this order: red, orange, yellow, green, blue, violet, purple, pink – then go neutral
- PRIORITISE YOUR FAVOURITES:
  Start with your favourite colour by shade
- BE PRACTICAL:
  Put into colours depending on those you wear the most
- MIX THINGS UP:
  Put outfits into colours for workwear and leisure; neutrals together with best colours
- GET CREATIVE:
  Put colourful prints, patterns or florals together, alongside block colours

Wardrobe warriors

We all need those pieces in our wardrobe that will fight for pole position and serve us purposefully all year round. Here's my take on what they are, but of course you might have others that win your battles for you. However, the first and most important factor is they have to be in your BEST COLOURS! Secondly, they have to take you from day to night, Winter to Summer and in between too. Lastly, they have to be able to be worn with lots of different items in your wardrobe to be sustainably brilliant and great investments.

The colourful scarf

I am not known as the Scarf Queen for nothing! I think colourful scarves deserve a whole book on their own because they are just THE best accessory for putting colour up against your complexion, for an instant facelift and mood boost. Here's why:

- If you are wearing a neutral outfit, a coloured scarf will give you that pop of colour that you need to make your skin glow and look healthy and attractive, without shouting about being overly 'bright'.
- A scarf can also take you from day to night, casual to smart in a jiffy.
- It definitely lifts the mood and look of a coat particularly in the colder months.
- Scarves can also be slimming – a coloured scarf will draw the eye instantly straight to it, plus if you wear one in a long shape it can elongate your body.
- Silk scarves can be tied at the neck for a smart workwear look with a dark outfit.
- Stoles and wraps not only keep you warm but add colour to a smart evening outfit.
- You can indulge in patterns, prints, florals or bold colours to highlight your personality if the rest of you is feeling beige.
- If you discover your new colour palette and want to introduce some small changes, get a scarf first.
- On a budget, a scarf is the perfect pick you up and doesn't have to be expensive.
- If you have an all-black wardrobe, scarves will be a welcome boost without having to make huge purchases.
- Love the idea but don't feel like wearing a scarf, then be uber fashionable and tie it round your bag so you get that

instant hit of happiness by looking at it!
• Wear them as headbands and head scarves too.

The essential jacket

As an item of clothing goes, I think this has to be the best wardrobe warrior for all-round versatility and wearability. Whether worn to work, or at leisure a neutral jacket will be your most sustainable piece; here's how to ensure you have one that succeeds in leading the way in your wardrobe:

• Choose navy, it's a classic, and there is a shade of navy blue that can be made to work for everyone; cool dark navy is best for Winters, soft navy for Summers, bright navy for Springs and marine navy for Autumns.
• Make sure it's good quality fabric for longevity.
• Don't buy into fashion unless it ticks all your boxes: best colour, best fit, goes with lots.
• Make sure your neutral jacket has either a warm base if you are Spring or Autumn, or a cool base if you are Summer or Winter.
• It needs to combine well with lots of things in your wardrobe: smarten it up with well-cut trousers/skirts/dresses; wear it casually with jeans/knitwear/T-shirts; wear it to work with a tie and a shirt.
• Think about your accessories and whether they can be teamed well with your chosen jacket.

Small colourful doses of optimism need their SPACE

Accessories:

Such an important part of creating your own sense of style and also a great way to inject a dose of optimism into your wardrobe with colour. Storing them so you can see the colours, patterns and fabrics at a glance by folding them up and rolling them means you grab what you want in an instant.

Scarves: either hang them with your coats/jacket so you know which ones work best together at a glance or store them in a drawer beautifully, or like me, use a coat stand! Other options are tie hangers or actual scarf holders and put them in your coat/jacket wardrobe, or hang on the back of a door. Silk scarves are lightweight and can be stored in drawers if you prefer.

Belts: tend to be neutral and can serve many a purpose. They can highlight a waist, they can elongate your legs, they can break up a long body. They smarten up a suit. Colourful belts can be a fab way to introduce a high fashion look to your outfit. Or allow you to indulge in wearing your favourite colour to match something else you are wearing, to make you look and feel well put together.

Ties: wearing a colourful tie is a fantastic way of expressing your personality, particularly if you wear a dark suit to work. The best way to see your colour choices in an instant is to hang ties in your wardrobe next to suits or workwear, and in colour order; block colours followed by stripes, patterns, florals and in your favourite colourways. If not, keep in a drawer that allows you instant access preferably with tie compartments so you can roll them up.

Gloves and hats: Winter warmers. Keep in drawers in matching sets if you can, and close to your coats. These days they come in lots of fun colourways with bobbles on the top, or embroidery, frills, sequins – go mad if that's your thing or stay simple in neutrals. For Summer caps and sombreros preferably store them with your swimwear so you know they are together.

Event hats: keep these in hat boxes if possible and up on high, on top of a wardrobe or locked in an attic. Please remember that hats reflect down on to your face and hair, so should always be in your best colours.

Headbands: these have become fashionable again and will probably keep doing the rounds, and they are fun ways to put a pop of colour into an otherwise neutral zone.

Bags: line them up or hang; neutrals then your palette colours, for instant access. Or put a smaller bag inside a big one. Evening/formal bags can be stored to keep them out of the way and kept in good condition.

Jewellery: you will know by now whether your best metals are cool or warm, and also what your colour palette is, so what stones will suit you, so keep your everyday jewellery close to hand and obviously lock up the really formal, expensive bits for best. You can store these by category, necklaces, bracelets, cufflinks, tiepins, brooches, or by colour depending on your preference. A colourful necklace is always a winner up against your face to put some harmony into your look and detract from a colour that might not be your most flattering.

Socks & tights: not strictly speaking 'accessories', more 'essentials' but these can be wonderful ways to put a pop of colour into an outfit, and to project your personality, when at work or having to wear a uniform. Keep them rolled up and in a drawer, preferably one with compartments, as you don't want to be spending your entire free time rerolling and folding. It's hard enough relocating pairs from the wash!

Pocket squares: a great way to inject some colour into a neutral or dark suit or blazer and go high end with some luxe silk, or plain cotton for a more casual look. Just remember of course to use the colours that suit you to highlight some of your fun characteristics.

Phone cases: be creative, see expert Stylist Peter's top tip below.

Expert Stylist Peter Kane's top tip for adding colour with accessories: "I've found that people who are scared of wearing colour can introduce their true colours in ephemeral items like purses, phone covers and bags. I once draped a lady who discovered through my analysis that she actually suited all the burnished Autumn tones, even though she arrived in head to toe black! When she brought out her phone, however, the cover was already in her best Autumn shades of orange and chocolate brown. We both started laughing."

Step 3: Focus on what you need

A budget and shopping list of necessary purchases

Your budget:
Focus on a budget, so as not to waste money, and only buy things that you need. If buying into the latest fashion, feel confident that the item will work hard for you in your new colour capsule wardrobe. Purchasing only your best colours from now on should save you money, because you don't need to make expensive mistakes ever again. This will ensure you start to build a more sustainable wardrobe from now on.

Your shopping list:
Now that your wardrobe has been cleared out and put back together in a new colourful way, it's much easier for you to see what's missing for your lifestyle. What I suggest is that you now go back to your wardrobe with a pen and a pad and note exactly where the gaps are. Write down a list of things you need to purchase:

- Replacements: what you have removed that served you well, but the wrong colour
- Essentials in your neutrals/colours: short/long-sleeved tees, collared shirts
- New shirts/tops for work (if needed) in your neutrals & colours
- New tops for fun, casual, lounging and/or going out in
- Jackets in your neutral shades for work and/or leisure, then coloured ones
- Work suits in your best neutrals
- Trousers/skirts that are functional for everyday life i.e., denim
- Trousers/skirts that are smart/formal
- Knitwear in your colour palette, lightweight or chunky
- Dresses that are a classic style, smart & casual, prints/patterns/florals
- Jumpsuits/tracksuits/hoodies/loungewear/athleticwear
- Shoes/boots/trainers in your best neutrals and colours
- Accessories: scarves, bags, belts, headbands, etc.
- Ties and pocket squares, socks and tights
- Coloured/metallic jewellery

You probably won't need all of the above, but it's helpful to have a checklist to focus on. Lists can of course be manipulated when out shopping if you fall in love with something in your colour palette that fits you well too. However, your initial one will be very helpful in focussing on which shops you need to visit, in person or online. The best way to get value for money and a level of sustainability is to weigh the cost of an item against the number of times you will wear it. Buying a jacket worth £150 that you use throughout the year is going to be much better value per wear than a cheaper one that you wear once or twice.

Sometimes it's actually better to just play it safe and purchase a classic timeless item. If you are going to splash out on an expensive classic, make sure it always belongs to your colour palette, be it either your best neutral or a colour you love. This is where so many wardrobes fail; full of colours that belong to someone else, don't resonate with that person at all and therefore don't get worn. If you do fall in love with a high fashion coloured item, that isn't in your best colour, make sure you can wear it well away from your face or accessorise it to pieces!

Expert Style Coach Janine Coney's top tip on affordable colour extras: "Think about ways you can elevate an outfit by buying a colourful bag, which can instantly put the wow into your look. A beautiful lipstick is inexpensive and will uplift your face in one of your best shades. A colourful scarf, tied elegantly, can totally light up your face. Once purchased, keep these accessories where you can easily see them every day!"

Step 4: Joyful shopping

In person or online; no more expensive mistakes!
Okay now be honest, do you hate shopping???? So many people do, and I really understand just how overwhelming it can be if you don't know where to begin. But now it's going to be different. You know your best colours and you are focussed with your list of what you need and want. Naturally, it's going to be easier to shop during the time of year that belongs to your seasonal palette.

If you are Spring in colouring and character then obviously buying things to suit you best in your bright warm palette will be in the shops during Springtime. Sales at the end of Spring are great to stock up with items you may need for the rest of the year. Come Winter, your colours may not be available in abundance, so you want to feel confident that you can still wear your own palette throughout the year, just maybe in more inventive ways!

Before heading off though, do think about fun ways you can shop in style. How about organising a colour-swap party? This is a great way to recycle clothing. You may end up with a bargain and also get some real joy knowing someone else will get to wear something of yours in a colour that never suited you but looks great on them!

My top tips for having fun and success OUT shopping:

- Plan your day and go where you will have the widest selection for your needs
- Shops tend to be emptier in the morning before lunchtime
- Go online 'colour scan-shopping' first, it saves time sourcing your shops
- If matching a colour for an outfit, take it with you to ensure accuracy
- Always wear comfortable shoes, trainers preferably, as walking for hours can be exhausting on the feet
- Wear some good underwear, consider what you might wear to an event
- Remember that lighting in shops can distort an item's true colours, so take things into the daylight if you possibly can without setting off shop alarms
- Make sure that you feel happy in your chosen colours when purchasing
- My top rule when trying out a new colour is to put it up against your face, blink and when you open your eyes see if the colour 'wears you' or is it in harmony with you
- Always check you can change or refund any colour purchase if it doesn't work as planned with other items in your wardrobe

Celebrity Fashion Stylist Phill Tarling's top tip for shopping colours: "My eyes are my colour checker. When I try something new on next to my face... if the peepers look lively, I am more likely to buy. If it makes me look a little tired, I walk away. Nothing that doesn't flatter is worth investing in."

The ONLINE option

Nowadays, we have become a world full of online shoppers. So, naturally retailers have had to get savvier at selling. This makes our lives easier to navigate stores and hopefully makes our shopping experience more pleasurable, as we can take more time. Many retailers have had to create virtual changing rooms and offer help in finding your size and even fit your body shape. Online shopping is also very beneficial if you can't face the idea of going to the shops in person. Or if for any reason you find yourself too busy working from home, with children or unable to leave, then going online is a fantastic alternative.

With your new-found colour knowledge buying online will be so much easier. There is also the thrill of the package turning up. My husband recently started working from home and said he was shocked that the courier seemed to know our dogs by name!!

One of the major benefits of online shopping is being able to try things on in the comfort of your own home. You can see how they look with other items in your wardrobe and put them together with accessories and shoes. So there is a lot to be said for this medium which has fast become a really enjoyable way to buy clothes.

My top tips for getting the best out of buying online:

- FEEL GOOD about giving back whilst online shopping by choosing brands that donate percentages of sales to charity.
- Spend time shopping around. You can visit several retail outlets in a matter of minutes from the comfort of your

own armchair, way faster than you could physically in person get round them all.

- Seek out PRE-LOVED sites. There are many available and you could save yourself a fortune and end up with a designer bargain and a sustainable beauty to boot!
- Do make sure you shop at reputable sites and check they are the right websites. Scamming is definitely a downside to online buying these days.
- Always check you know what the returns policy is; how long you have before the item needs to be returned for a refund if you don't like it.
- Know whether the return is freepost or you have to pay postage (particularly if buying abroad) which might mean having to go to a post office.
- Sizing can be a real problem when most shops vary so much, check out the measurements before you purchase or if unsure then buy two sizes with the view to sending one back.

Whichever way you shop the most important thing is to remember to enjoy yourself!!!!

Expert Stylist Angela Hathway's top tip for shopping well:
"Take things slowly and be more conscious when shopping. Think how hard each purchase will work for you, how the colour will make you feel, and will it mix easily with existing pieces you own? Knowing your best colours is a lifetime tool, which means you can shop with ease; no more mistakes and throwaway items. Identify those perfect pieces, knowing they will have a place in your wardrobe for more than one season."

Chapter 5

Put the *Wow* into your workwear

Dress confidently for your profession
What colours to wear to an interview
Light up the screen on virtual meetings online
Best colours to wear at work and why
Prescribe your own colour confident work wardrobe
Spring – Autumn – Summer – Winter at work

The workplace is changing. Over the years corporate companies have become more colourful and casual. How empowering it can be to express your individuality and authentic self, by wearing your best colours to impress, feel confident and look good. Many of you will now be working from home, which like most things in life has its positives and its pitfalls. One thing that remains constant, though, is making sure you always look and feel your best at work, whether it's physically in person or virtually online.

In this chapter, I want to take the stress out of business dressing, so you are free to be your best at work. Imagine all your neutrals and colour outfits, ready to wear, alone or combined in your new colour capsule wardrobe. Save yourself time and money, with workwear that is appropriate for your job, whilst highlighting your personality.

Ridley London founder & designer Camilla Ridley's top tip for empowerment in the workplace: *"Traditionally, the workplace has been dominated by monochrome, particularly in more corporate male centric environments. However, workwear is relaxing to reflect a cultural shift introducing a greater variety of colour and print, highlighting qualities like individuality, creativity and empathy* *increasingly seen as drivers of success. From the traditional codes of two-piece power dressing to the modern-day versatility of the printed dress, thus creating a more individualised, progressive look, and worn with a jacket, or cardigan for a relaxed appearance. As the logic seamlessly follows, if you feel more relaxed, comfortable and confident in your appearance you will undoubtedly perform better."*

You never get a second chance to make a first impression:
You have between 10-40 seconds to impress with your appearance.

- Whether you are in a meeting at work, at a job interview or going for a promotion, first impressions are critical and you need to be memorable for the right reasons.
- Your appearance, for right or wrong, is the first thing seen before you say a word.
- Always wear your best colours to project your personality and feel confident.
- Dressing to impress is just as important virtually online as it is in person.

Dress confidently for your profession:

The aim: to always look your best; feel confident and calm, knowing you are wearing the colours that suit you, whilst appearing professional when needed. This means dressing appropriately for the job, whilst highlighting your personality and natural talent.

Below is a brief look at industry dress codes in a colourful way. Of course, this is by no means comprehensive, simply a guide to help you think about what to wear within your chosen profession or an interview. Research the industry/company first, and if necessary, ring up an HR department if they have one to check the dress code.

Corporate:

- Smart trouser/skirt/dress suits in neutrals or darker shades of colours, block, or with patterns/prints
- Well-cut blazers and/or trousers in neutral or conservative colours
- Neutral or light-coloured shirts
- Coloured tailored tops
- Colours generally should err more on the conservative side
- Dresses/skirts in colours that are not overly bright or tight
- Ties, pocket handkerchiefs in colours, designs that project your personality
- Black/brown/navy or neutral-coloured shoes & bags/briefcases/accessories

Finance:

- Trouser/skirt/dress suits in dark neutral shades, block, or subtle patterns and prints
- A dark black/navy blue/grey suit is authoritative
- A knee-length tailored dress or skirt/trousers in a neutral colour
- Tailored, fitted jacket in a colour of choice
- White or soft/pastel-coloured collared shirts
- Accessories smart and in classic, conservative colours
- Ties and pocket handkerchiefs should be conservative but can be colourful
- Black/navy shoes are best, brown is acceptable

Tech:

- Wearing a dark suit may be overdressed, a lighter colour might be more appropriate

- Blazer/shirt and well-cut trousers/skirt/dress in colours & patterns of choice
- Accessories/shoes/trainers casual and in colours in your seasonal palette

Creative:

- Tonal dressing is fun with your chosen colours and consider colour clashing
- Casual trousers; dark blue, denim or black
- Tops and ties in colours to suit you but preferably one item i.e., blazer or shirt
- Dresses/skirts in fun colours and patterns/florals
- Coloured trainers/loafers/sandals
- Shirts can be in bold colours, or patterns/florals
- Shoes/trainers and socks can be colourful

Fashion:

- Allow yourself to be super trendy with a colourful streak
- Go bright and vibrant if it's part of your seasonal palette
- Clothes stylish and colourful to show off your personality
- Make accessories a focal fun point of colour and style
- Colour combine, clash, harmonise, go bold, patterned or printed
- Colourful shoes/trainers, socks, ties, a sharp bag, modern jewellery display your taste

What colours to wear to an interview and why:

RED means power, drive and enthusiasm, will get you noticed and shows you have the drive to get things done; best for advertising/marketing, sales, PR and the law, but can be worn in small amounts for all industries, and great combined with neutral shades for balance, and particularly blue for balance.

ORANGE is confident and sociable, friendly and adventurous; best for sales/marketing/PR but in its softer, paler shades can be combined with blue, grey and brown for all industries.

YELLOW is the colour of clarity, assurance and positivity, mentally stimulating and uplifting; best for creative industries, fashion and media, and in small amounts for all industries.

GREEN is the colour of balanced and clear decision making, humanitarian and harmonious; best for creative industries, but a good fit for most businesses, as it aids all productivity.

BLUE is the safest option for interviews: best for corporate/ sales; represents trust, reliability and good communication, and helps to keep you calm, so a great choice for all industries and lots of shades to choose from for everyone, with navy being the most 'serious'.

PURPLE is the colour of creativity, inspiration and mediation, and is calming; best for artistic pursuits and law, fashion and media, and in small amounts for all industries.

PINK is supportive and compassionate, kind and fun-loving: best for the caring industries, fashion and media; combined with dark neutrals can be worn in all industries.

BROWN is traditional, conservative, grounded; best as an alternative to 'black', and camel/beige/taupe good in all industries and mixes well with other colours.

BLACK conveys leadership and authority; best for managerial positions, and corporate/finance companies; represents authority and discipline and suits the Winter season.

GREY is professional, practical and dignified with fair judgement; a great neutral for all industries.

WHITE/CREAM are traditional, reassuring and orderly; great choices for all industries, especially in the Summer months and allow other colours to shine.

Consider the importance of light and dark shades at work:

- Darker shades of clothing appear to be more formal and show authority
- Lighter shades come across as friendly and also approachable
- Brighter bolder shades tend to highlight a confident and fun-loving nature (think hot pink versus pastel)
- Muted shades can be used in a more conservative way
- Contrasting shades like navy and white project an air of authority

Expert Stylist Sarah Thomson's top tip on wearing colour for public speaking: "If you need a boost for public speaking experiment with shades of red to project an image of confidence and passion and to create an aura of excitement about your subject. I love to combine red with purple to add some inspiring balance into the mix, highlighting trust, creativity, whilst the addition of blue helps to keep you feeling calm."

The importance of projecting an individual, positive IMAGE

There are pitfalls to consider these days when creating a business image. Strict rules have given way to more flexible guidelines, in some professions. Moving away from the "traditional power suit" to the more smart-casual outfits of well-cut separates and accessories. But the message is still the same, your appearance matters, whether the rules apply or not.

- Dress according to your own individual colours and express your personality, feel confident and always look your best
- Be image appropriate for the industry and business you have chosen to work in

- Consider who you are meeting – presenting to – communicating with
- Create a capsule business wardrobe to suit YOU, and it will be the best investment you will ever make
- Consider adding colourful accessories, they can put your personality on display in small, effective ways

Expert Stylist Millie Coates' top tip for transforming workwear with colour: "Workwear doesn't need to (and really shouldn't!) be boring. A dark suit can be transformed by wearing a statement necklace, collar or colourful silk neck scarf. Alternatively, swap the more traditional outfit for a midi dress in a bold print and/or colour and pair with a smart black or navy blazer and heels. And a finishing touch of lipstick is a simple fix to elevate any outfit. The key is to look professional whilst letting your personality shine through – it will energise you and make your workday that much brighter, I guarantee."

Colours at work – how things have changed

There is no question that over the past few years, things have gone more casual in the workplace. Where ties were the norm, nowadays they are often cast into the desk drawer until the next meeting takes place. Thankfully there are now more options available than the obligatory white work shirt.

So, welcome into your wardrobe a colourful shirt or two. Also take time to pay attention to the colour of your scarves, ties, socks, tights and pocket handkerchiefs if you use them! These can be bright, bold, stripy, floral or patterned. They are fabulous ways to express your personality, especially if you are having to wear a suit to work. You will have discovered your prescribed colour palette in the book, and it is safe to say that in most work environments the softer, pastel shades of your best seasonal colours will always be appropriate. Just stick to your warm or cool rules.

Expert Stylist Clare Watkins' top tip for boosting colourful classics at work: "*No one should be afraid to add colour to their wardrobes, as it impacts everyone. By wearing colour, you also avoid blending into the crowd. Try pairing colour with something classic that you know suits you to instantly elevate your look. Get creative with the lining of your suit, add a colourful shirt, pocket square or tie, have your collar or shirt cuffs lined with a colourful or patterned fabric or be bold and wear a block colour under a classic blazer... the options are endless.*"

Please wear PINK!

Back in 2016, Pantone, a global authority for colour communication and inspiration worldwide, brought out their 'Color of the Year' that happened to be a blend of two colours namely 'Rose Quartz' a soft shade of pink, and 'Serenity' a delicate blue. This was a powerful message to the world, crossing cultural and gender boundaries, in fashion and interiors. I am delighted to see that over the past few years retail sales of pink shirts have grown hugely, and it's a real joy to see shades of pink at work, rather than defaulting to trusty blue. Whilst always a fabulous colour choice as blue represents trust, diplomacy and good communication, I think it's great that pink is now becoming a colourful option for everyone, to incorporate into workwear.

Expert Stylist Jacqueline Lythe's top tip for embracing pink at work: "*Pink has finally been freed from the realm of girly-girl, and rightfully been embraced by the fashion-world as a timeless and classic colour for men as well as women. Be brave when combining varied hues of pink and put thought into your accessories: ties, pocket handkerchiefs and yes socks, as these tiny details have the power to transform a look, particularly where pink is concerned.*"

Dress to be authentically YOU

When dressing for business consider what colours harmonise with your skin tone, eye and hair colour to give you the confidence to look and feel your best at work. Ensure you stand out for your individuality and natural talents. Your appearance reflects your personality as well as the company you work for, so mindfully choose the colours of your outfits.

The money spent on your working wardrobe should be considered a long-term investment in yourself and your career. If you wear suits or blazers to work, get these colours right first, then choose shirts/tops in your softer palette shades or whatever white or off-white belongs to your palette. Then consider your trousers/skirts/dresses followed by accessories, scarves, belts, coloured ties, socks and pocket handkerchiefs (if you use them).

Black, navy and grey are classic workwear colours, but bear in mind black belongs only to the cool Winter palette and that navy and grey will either have a cool or a warm base to consider, so some will suit you better than others. Classic brown and green suits are more often seen as appropriate for work in a country environment.

Accessories are where you can indulge in expressing your fashionable flair, and should always be in your best colours. Taking control of the colours in your wardrobe will be hugely rewarding for your career and success for the future.

Every day consider your role: if you are communicating to lots of people and need to inspire them to action, think about incorporating some red into your workwear and blue; exerting your authority then consider black (if it's in your palette), dark blue or grey, along with your best neutrals; if your mediation skills are needed then add some purple into the mix.

Expert Stylist Nick Hems' top tip for not shouting in colour:
"It might not always be appropriate or work to wear bright pink or neon green on the outside during the day, but we know colour impacts

our mood, so there's nothing to stop us wearing it underneath. As someone that has spent years playing with and styling a multitude of accessories for myself from hats, scarves, cufflinks, socks, bracelets and the list goes on, I now find the simplest thing I can do is wear a good pair of boxers in a vibrant colour and that proves to be the best way to set me up for a good day."

Light up the screen on virtual meetings online

For right or wrong, we are all judged on our appearance within the first few seconds of meeting/seeing us, so consider the instant impact you are making. Being on screen in colours that suit you, that make you look healthy and express your personality, can enhance your image. This helps you to feel more confident and in control, for all virtual work meetings (and interviews).

As you are being seen mainly from the waist or neck up, your complexion and face are going to be the focus of attention. By wearing your true colours up against your face, you will ensure you always look fabulous, as self-care and self-esteem are intrinsically linked. Revert back to the Colour chapter in this book if you need to establish your seasonal colour palette.

What you want to be seen:

- An even complexion
- A healthy look
- Glowing skin
- Less need for make-up
- Sparkling whites of your eyes
- Looking youthful
- A smiling face

What you don't want to be seen:

- A tired panda-eyed look

- Lines, wrinkles or distinctive signs of ageing
- A washed-out and unhealthy appearance
- Blotchy skin
- Red patches highlighted on the skin
- A double chin
- Dark roots in your hair
- Looking like you need to put on lots of make-up or concealer

You can get yourself dressed in the most fabulous outfit but get the lighting or the positioning of the camera wrong, and you may end up looking washed out and exhausted, or having your nostrils examined instead! Being 'camera ready' at all times is important, and setting the scene in your home for a work meeting (or interview) will save you time and keep you calm knowing you are ready to go. It's important to feel confident that you look and feel great and that your background is supporting you in the best way possible for ultimate success in your job.

My top tech tips:

Lighting is key

- A window will reflect your best appearance if it's in front of you and not behind
- Natural light is always advisable against artificial ones in a room
- Invest in a couple of natural daylight bulbs if natural light is not possible
- Position two lamps either side of your computer/laptop/ phone rather than one
- Beware of the glare of wearing glasses by not putting light directly in front of you

Position

- Make sure the camera on any device you are using is at your eye level
- Put laptop/phone on books or a stand to get to this eye level
- Use an adjustable device for flexibility

Location

- Choose the best room/location that reflects the meeting you are having
- Don't appear invisible, ensure you wear colours that make you the focal point
- Make sure your background is simple and tidy
- If you are having a more relaxed meeting, it's fine to have some colour in your background, or go outside into nature

Sound

- Ensure you are in a space that is as noise free as possible
- Turn off all phones
- If you have animals, put them in another room
- If you are expecting a delivery, think ahead, and let them know, or put a sign on your door with instructions not to ring the bell

My top colour tips for getting camera ready

- Get four of your best colourful work outfits camera ready in your wardrobe
- Dress appropriately for the online meeting/interview that day
- Consider which colours psychologically will enhance

your performance for the meeting: if you need some
energy and drive, choose red; good mediation skills,
choose purple

- Stand out in your best colours and don't be overpowered
  by your surroundings
- Don't disappear by wearing colours that blend in with
  your walls
- Consider (if you wear it) putting on make-up in colours
  that harmonise with your individual skin tone; you will
  be easier to connect with looking colourful
- Always appear fully dressed wearing appropriate shirts/
  tops and/or jackets
- Wear bottoms (with a belt if needed), either a stylish pair
  of trousers, skirt or a dress, you never know when you
  might have to get up and fetch something
- Mindfully choose your best colours to reflect your
  personality as well as making your skin glow, and don't
  always default to wearing black
- If wearing a plain, neutral outfit, consider colourful
  accessories, ties, jewellery; earrings and necklaces
- Colourful collars are a great way to put some vital colour
  up against your face

Expert Stylist Charlotte Broadbent's top tip on how to communicate your best self virtually: *"Severing ties with moody, bleak blacks and gloomy greys in your virtual work wardrobe catapults you into a world of 'mood boosting' colours, like red which releases adrenaline into your system and yellow which instils positivity and optimism. One of my business clients had a catalytic moment when she discovered her best, most appropriate colours for different corporate audiences is the secret ingredient to how others perceive us. She felt that wearing her most flattering colours now reflects who she wants to be, choosing specific colours as a powerful communication tool being important for first impressions."*

Prescribe your own colour confident work wardrobe

SPRING at work

Spring is a bright, warm palette, highlighting the hotter end of the spectrum; reds, corals, yellows. Consider going softer into Spring's pastel shades if you need to tone things down:

- Red: Bright, poppy, scarlet, pillar box, mango, bright red orange
- Yellow: Bright, daffodil, clear golden
- Green: Bright, lime, bright emerald, blue-green, aqua
- Blue: Bright, turquoise, periwinkle, light navy, electric
- Pink: Bright, hot, coral, salmon
- Orange: Bright, mango, apricot, peach, coral
- Purple: Bright purple, bright violet, lilac
- Brown: Camel, warm stone, golden brown, tan
- Neutrals: Bright navy, warm grey, cream, ivory, gold

Spring's best workwear colour combinations:

- *Bright navy blue & aqua/turquoise:* Combine good communication, whilst highlighting your ability to be trustworthy, reliable and dependable, whilst also having an upbeat and fun side to your character.
- *Bright navy blue & poppy red:* Combine good communication, whilst highlighting your ability to be trustworthy, reliable and dependable, whilst also having a passion for the job and the drive to get it done.
- *Bright navy blue & emerald green:* Combine good communication, whilst highlighting your ability to be trustworthy, reliable and dependable, whilst also having a balanced approach to work, able to see all sides of the situation clearly and make impartial decisions.
- *Warm grey & yellow:* Combine a practical, professional

and clear-headed approach to work, whilst also having a creative, positive outlook.

- *Warm grey & bright blue:* Combine a practical, professional and clear-headed approach to work, whilst also having good communication skills, whilst highlighting your ability to be trustworthy, reliable and dependable.
- *Warm grey & purple:* Combine a practical, professional and clear-headed approach to work, with a creative mind, someone who is a good mediator and inspires others. Add in some orange for extra warmth, and sociability, or pink to show an independent and compassionate spirit.

ACCESSORIES: any of the above combinations can be mixed with the following:

- *Bags; briefcases; belts; shoes:* camel, warm stone, tan, bright navy, warm grey, cream, ivory, peach, gold metallics.
- *Scarves, ties and socks:* in any of your bright, warm, Spring shades!
- *Jewellery:* bright gold, stones of turquoise, orange, red or emerald.

NB: Your palette does NOT include Black. However, if you choose to wear it at work (or for an interview) please keep it away from your face and wear in moderation, with one of your best Spring colours, or neutrals.

AUTUMN at work

Autumn is a very warm, muted and earthy palette, highlighting the yellow/golden hotter end of the spectrum. Instead of black you have many warm brown shades to choose from so combine with your reds, oranges and golds, and consider differing shades of the following:

- Red: Orange-red, rust, brick, bittersweet, warm tomato red
- Yellow: Mustard, golden, tan, camel
- Green: Jade, yellow-green, dark lime
- Blue: Teal, marine, muted turquoise
- Pink: Dark salmon, dark peach, muted pink
- Orange: True orange, dark apricot, coral, mango, deep peach, terracotta
- Purple: Muted purple
- Brown: Coffee, bronze, camel, honey, warm beige, caramel, chocolate
- Neutrals: warm browns, marine navy, military grey, coffee-cream, ivory, cream

Autumn's best workwear colour combinations:

- *Teal blue and chocolate:* Combine good communication, whilst highlighting your ability to be trustworthy, reliable and dependable, and help to keep you feeling grounded and show you are down to earth.
- *Camel and cream:* Combine a traditional and conservative look, whilst helping to keep you feeling grounded and show you are down to earth, with a realistic approach that shows an ability to be objective.
- *Military grey and jade green:* Combine a practical, professional and clear-headed approach to work, whilst also having a balanced approach, being able to see all sides of the situation clearly and make impartial decisions.
- *Mustard yellow and khaki green:* Combine an air of clarity and assurance, along with an optimistic nature, whilst also showing you have a balanced approach, being able to see all sides of the situation clearly and make impartial decisions.
- *Marine blue and rust red:* Combine good communication,

whilst highlighting your ability to be trustworthy, reliable and dependable, also having a passion for the job and the drive to get it done.

- *Burnt orange and warm beige:* Combine a naturally confident and outgoing nature, with a traditional, down-to-earth, practical outlook.
- *Dark khaki green and peach:* Combine your naturally balanced approach to work, being able to see all sides of the situation clearly and able to make impartial decisions in a naturally confident and outgoing way.

ACCESSORIES: any of the above combinations can be mixed with the following:

- *Bags; briefcases; belts; shoes:* all shades of warm brown; coffee, bronze, camel, honey, beige, caramel, chocolate, peach; marine navy; military grey; coffee-cream; dark gold, bronze metallics.
- *Scarves, ties and socks:* in any of your warm, earthy Autumn shades.
- *Jewellery:* antique gold, bronze, stones in teal, orange, jade, amber, tiger's eye.

NB: Your palette does NOT include Black. However, if you choose to wear it to work (or an interview), please keep it away from your face and wear in moderation, with one of your best Autumn colours, or neutrals.

SUMMER at work

Summer is a light, cool and delicate colour palette. Highlighting the cooler end of the spectrum, blues, pinks and purples in particular, so consider any shades of the following:

- Red: Raspberry, watermelon, light burgundy

- Yellow: Light lemon
- Green: Mint, light emerald
- Blue: Powder blue, light aqua, periwinkle, muted turquoise, cadet, muted navy, blue-grey
- Pink: Rose, carnation, pastel, powder pink, light muted pink, pale fuchsia & magenta
- Orange: Muted soft peach
- Purple: Muted purple, lavender, violet, lilac
- Brown: Taupe, almond, rose beige
- Neutrals: Navy blue, dove grey, silver-grey, mid-charcoal grey, blue-grey

Summer's best workwear colour combinations:

- *Muted navy with mint green:* Combines good communication through your diplomatic nature, you are trustworthy, reliable and dependable, whilst also having a balanced approach to work, able to see all sides of the situation clearly and make impartial decisions.
- *Mid-grey with raspberry red:* Combines a practical, professional and clear-headed approach to work, whilst also having a passion for the job and the drive to get it done.
- *Muted navy with lavender:* Combines your diplomacy through communication, and ability to be trustworthy, reliable and dependable with a creative mind; someone who is a good mediator and a great listener.
- *Mid-grey with pale magenta:* Combines a practical, professional and clear-headed approach to work whilst highlighting an independent, fun-loving spirit who is supportive and compassionate towards others.
- *Dove grey with periwinkle blue:* Combines a practical, professional and clear-headed approach to work, whilst highlighting your diplomatic nature and ability to be

trustworthy, reliable and dependable.

- *Cool beige with powder blue:* Combines a down-to-earth, hands-on approach whilst highlighting your diplomatic nature, and your ability to be trustworthy, reliable and dependable.

ACCESSORIES: any of the above combinations can be mixed with the following:

- *Bags; briefcases; belts; shoes:* navy blue, dove grey, silver-grey, mid-charcoal grey, blue-grey, taupe, almond, rose beige, silver metallics.
- *Scarves, ties and socks:* in any combination of your soft, delicate pastel shades.
- *Jewellery:* silver & pearls, plus stones in pale pink (rose crystal), blue and purple (amethyst).

NB: Your palette does NOT include Black. However, if you choose to wear it to work (or an interview) please keep it away from your face and wear in moderation, with one of your best Summer colours, or neutrals.

WINTER at work

Yes, you can wear black better than all of the other seasons. Whilst this is an authoritative work colour, it really does 'mean business', so choose how much you wear with care. You can also opt for one of your 'neutrals' and add one or two of your vibrant shades into the mix in any of the following cool shades:

- Red: Blue red, true red, cool bright red, burgundy red, maroon
- Pink: Fuchsia, magenta, plum, hot cool pink, icy pastel pink
- Blue: Bright cool turquoise, Chinese blue, cobalt, electric,

icy pastel blue, dark navy
- Green: Pine, emerald, dark jade, pastel green
- Purple: Blue-violet, royal, ultraviolet, deep purple
- Yellow: Acid, neon, icy pastel yellow
- Grey: Charcoal, grey-black, silver-grey, icy pastel grey
- Neutrals: Black-brown, navy blue, charcoal grey, taupe, white, pastel grey

Winter's best workwear colour combinations:

- *Black and cobalt blue:* Combine a sense of authority and discipline with good communication skills and an ability to get the job done with integrity and reliability.
- *Black and burgundy red:* Combine a sense of authority and discipline whilst also having a passion for the job and the drive to get it done.
- *Black and ultraviolet:* Combine a sense of authority and discipline whilst highlighting your ability to be dependable with a creative mind. Someone who is a good mediator and inspires others.
- *Black and white:* Combine a sense of authority and discipline with impartiality and fairness of judgement, being objective and clear thinking.
- *Black and fuchsia pink:* Combine a sense of authority and discipline with a supportive and compassionate nature, whilst showing a fun-loving and independent spirit.
- *Black and neon yellow:* Combine a sense of authority and discipline with a creative and optimistic nature.
- *Navy blue and icy cool green:* Combine good communication skills and an ability to get the job done with integrity whilst also having a balanced approach to work. Able to see all sides of a discussion clearly and make impartial decisions.
- *Charcoal grey and pastel blue:* Combine a practical,

professional and clear-headed approach to work with good communication, whilst highlighting your ability to stay calm in any situation.

ACCESSORIES: any of the above combinations can be mixed with the following:

- *Bags; briefcases; belts; shoes:* black, charcoal, grey-black, silver-grey, black-brown, navy blue, taupe, white, pastel grey, silver metallics.
- *Scarves, ties and socks:* try and keep things simple, no more than two or three colours.
- *Jewellery:* silver, platinum, diamonds, and stones with icy cool/vibrant coloured stones.

Expert Stylist Aoife Duncan's top tip for wearing colour to work: "I advise my clients to ask themselves two questions before they get dressed in the morning. Firstly, how do they want to feel: energetic, calm, confident? Secondly, who do they need to impress, a new client, a new boss? Someone who wants to feel confident and trustworthy might choose the powerful combination of adrenaline-releasing red with communicative blue. Another may need to stand up and energise a room in front of a hundred people, then it's red all the way. Choosing colours in this way, puts you in the driving seat and allows you to take control of your mood and consciously steer the outcome of a situation."

Chapter 6

Comfort and Convenience – dressing in colour

Trend up your leisurewear
Rejoice in comfort dressing – Feel nice in neutrals
Cosy-up in calm colours
Elevate your everyday outfits & lighten the mood
Prescribe your own seasonal comfort colours
Spring – Autumn – Summer – Winter comfort zones

Trend up your leisurewear

Recent times have given growth to the latest trend in comfort dressing. Whether you fancy going out to grab a paper in silk pyjamas, curl up on the sofa to watch a movie in a 'nap' dress (yup it's a thing!), or do some housework in a tracksuit, comfort clothing is currently big business. It's popular and so we need to give it book space.

The biggest new wave in casual clothing, amongst others, is known among fashionistas as athleisure wear. This in a nutshell is gym stuff that is fast becoming wardrobe staples. Being casual is definitely part of the recent staying in, and who doesn't want to feel fabulously at ease and comfortable in their clothing choices? Isn't it a wonderful excuse to be sloppy and unkempt? No, it really isn't. This is a new way to be fashionable, to feel relaxed and wear clothing that feels lovely; loose but not tight and restrictive but physically at ease. Maybe in a luxe fabric, and importantly we need to consider colours that make you feel calm, balanced, and really comfortable wearing.

In challenging times, it's more important than ever to invest in your own self-care and well-being. A balanced lifestyle comes from feeling happy. So, we need to discuss comfort colours, and how to stay out of the 'all grey zone', as this can help to lighten your mood, whatever the weather, at home or outward bound.

Rejoice in comfort dressing

There are many variations of 'comfort dressing' and the joy of this trend is of course pleasing yourself to one or many of the items I am about to list. Colour plays a huge part in keeping your energy up. So whatever style of casual clothing you choose to wear, check your best colours before you purchase. The idea is to look comfy and chic on and off your yoga mat!

Here are some 'fashionable' suggestions for you to consider, before we talk 'colour'. You may already have some of these in your wardrobe, and if you do consider wearing them out as well as in, maybe colour combine them to update this new trend.

Comfortable essentials:
Stylish tracksuits
Tracksuit bottoms
Kimono or plain wraps
Slouchy knitwear
Longline cardigans
Sweatshirt tops/hoodies
Long sleeve/oversize tees
Pyjama-style tops and bottoms
Jumpsuits
Joggers/cargos
Leggings
Shorts
Trainers

Comfortable extras:
Puffa jackets
Ankle boots
Jersey dresses

Feel nice in neutrals

Kettlewell Colours founder Melissa Nicholson's top tip on feeling nice in neutrals: "Knowing your neutrals is like baking the best possible sponge cake before getting on with the decoration. Start with navy, grey or stone and then add your best colour pop in a scarf or top close to your face."

Why be neutral? It's easy, practical, no nonsense and never goes out of fashion. BUT please remember everyone has good and bad neutrals, ones that either have a cool or a warm base and if you want to keep your complexion looking healthy and attractive, even if you are in your comfort zone, then do take note of my seasonal sections below. Firstly, here is a quick precis of the psychological effects of wearing an ALL-neutral outfit in your comfort zone.

BLACK means hide and protect. Yup it's great if that's your intention and it makes you happy, then hide away. Black is no nonsense, means business, speaks of control. However, if you have read the seasonal chapters in this book, you will also know that I do not prescribe wearing black to anyone other than a Winter type, and those of you who have strong cool influences. But, if you love it as I know lots of you do, particularly in the Winter months, then remember to try and put one of your best colours up against your face i.e., a polo neck, scarf or tee with it. Beware the energy drain from wearing all black for long periods of time and of course the tired panda-eyed look... eek!

GREY is practical, efficient and workable into any wardrobe, and comes in many light and dark shades. Grey is basically the combination of black and white. However, the addition of some yellow or red to grey's base warms it up and a blue base makes it uber-cool. Psychologically grey is impartial and projects detachment, but there is a danger that it can appear unfriendly and aloof if worn in abundance. So, it's a great colour if you need some space, or want to spend time alone. Beware being in grey for too long and always consider combining with a colour that helps you feel more upbeat.

BROWN is stabilising, grounding and helps to keep you centred. Brown is actually what's known as a composite colour i.e., one that is made by mixing other colours together. Where black and grey favour cool skin tones, Springs and particularly Autumns look lovely in the warmer shades of brown; the caramels, toffees, tans and chestnuts. Cooler taupe and almond browns with pink bases will suit the Summer/Winter types better. So, whilst brown psychologically helps to harness the safety and structure of the earth, too much can stop you from getting active, so balance your browns with a chosen colour.

WHITE and CREAM are lovely neutrals particularly in the Summertime, but there are no rules to say that they can't be worn in Winter too! Not hugely practical if you have a family or pets, as they show the dirt big time. But there is something very fresh and clean about putting on cashmere cream to feel luxurious and warm in. These are clarifying colours that help you feel optimistic and create space if you need it. Also providing you with a blank canvas to cosy up in and help you feel balanced too.

A lot of this loungewear trend happens to be in black and grey and other neutrals. Whilst there is nothing against wearing monochrome or dark coloured clothing, there is science that suggests these colours (or lack of rainbow colours), whilst feeling protective and allowing you to have your 'invisible' moments, don't let in the light!

Expert Stylist Laura Tippett-Wilson's top tip on adding colour to neutrals: "Happiness for me is as easy as adding colour to an outfit. So, my top tip is to always wear a pop of your favourite bright colours underneath your neutrals, like vibrant red under a navy coat. Uplifting your dark neutrals with colour always sets you up for a brighter day."

Cosy-up in calm colours

Due to their shorter wavelengths of light, the cooler and more calming of the rainbow colours are green, blue and violet. In challenging times of stress or fear, they can have pacifying effects on our senses. These physically help to reduce blood pressure and calm the nervous system, so wonderful to wear if you are feeling particularly anxious. Beneficial when meditating or needing to get into a peaceful and reflective zone. Cooler colours on the spectrum could also aid in good sleep which in turn can help keep your immune system healthy.

GREEN is midway on the colour spectrum so gets warmer with the addition of yellow, or cooler with blue. Either way, green represents harmony and balance which may well be needed when dealing with relations or friends. Green is about renewal and fresh beginnings, so a wonderful colour to consider in your comfort zone if starting a new project or hobby. Go softer and more pastel if you choose, depending on your palette of course. There are lots of lovely green shades of mint, pistachio, jade, emerald, lime and sea green. Green harmonises happily with compassionate pink.

BLUE is all about feeling calm, so a valuable colour choice in your comfortable attire. Turquoise shades suit everyone and are youthful and fun-loving. With the pale pastels being more appropriate for the cooler tones and teals for warm. Team with yellow to freshen blue up or pink to elevate the fun. Navy is another good choice in this arena, and can be great to divert from wearing black, but try not to wear too much at one time, and combine with a favourite colour.

Shades of **PURPLE & VIOLET** are the perfect comfort colours to assist with all 'mediation' at home or at work, to wear in your comfort clothing. Also fabulous for calming meditations and yoga sessions. Shades include lilac and lavender, particularly lovely in the Summer months.

PINK can be a combo of red and white or red and blue,

which turns it magenta. I am including it because it's such an important colour, gentler than red, and associated with love and compassion. A gorgeous colour for feeling comfortable in your own skin. There are many shades of pink to choose from, so make sure you are in the right seasonal palette; cooler pinks will be shades of raspberry, fuchsia and rose; coral and salmon pinks belong to warmer skin tones. Pink is a fabulous colour choice for everyone, as it represents nurturing and love. In these times we find ourselves in, it's so important to show kindness for one another, and to be caring of mother earth.

Your emotions and lifestyle situations will probably determine how you feel and which colours you want to wear on a daily basis. Go with your internal flow. Maybe today you need to wear an abundance of one chosen 'bright' colour. Perhaps tomorrow you will need to be in a neutral zone. The following day may open up a colourful combination to you.

Consider how wonderful it is that you can give yourself a hit of rainbow light and also open up powerful possibilities of self-discovery and personal growth at the same time. Take control of your own emotions and turn any challenging situation into a positive time to learn something new, feel calmer, more balanced and happier.

Expert Stylist Karina Morin's top tip for some calm and healing:
"Cool colours like blues and greens have a very healing effect on your psyche. When you're in need of some self-care surround yourself in these colours and observe how at ease you feel. Just like walking in a forest on a sunny day with the green trees and blue sky, it can be quite therapeutic."

Elevate your everyday outfits & lighten the mood

All the fun of family and friends:
Eating together: Stimulating oranges and reds, blue for

	communication
Relaxing:	Calming blues and balancing greens, meditative purple
Playing with kids:	Joyful and mentally creative yellow
School reunion:	Feel confident and have fun in yellow or sociable orange
Meet the in-laws:	Blue for reliability and trustworthiness, purple for mediation

Activities:

Exercise:	Adrenaline releasing, energy boosting reds, orange and yellow
Hobbies:	Get started with something new and be productive with green
Meditating:	Find a deep relaxing space with the power of purple or cool blue

Socialising:

First date:	Be approachable and combine romantic red or compassionate pink
	with trusting blue for great communication or protective black, to keep
	things hidden till the next date
An evening out:	Think happy, fun-loving colours like reds, oranges, yellows and pinks
	along with turquoise to get everyone laughing and chatting

Lighten the mood in your comfort zone

Rainbow colours and happiness

We all need light. If in any doubt please reread the earlier chapter on colour and its scientific effects. Some of you may have heard of the English scientist Isaac Newton (1642-1727), as he famously made an amazing discovery. When he shone sunlight through a glass prism, he noted the rainbow of colours which became known as the 'colour spectrum'. This was made up of the seven key colours, namely: red, orange, yellow, green, blue, indigo and violet.

Often, we can be unaware of the subconscious way the rainbow of colours has an effect on us. We are of course all different, and therefore the impact a colour can have varies, both physically and emotionally. Generally, we will feel the hotter colours of the rainbow spectrum like red, orange and yellow being more stimulating to our senses.

Get active in your comfort zone

Due to their long wavelengths of light, the hottest colours red, orange and yellow have the ability to stimulate and excite, encouraging us into a new venture or project. They can be experienced as uplifting, raising energy levels and motivating us to action; to get busy or start a new exercise plan. This is thanks to our visual sight and hormones reacting to these hotter colours that can give us that instant 'hit' of positivity, making us smile and get moving.

RED is a primary colour and the hottest most stimulating of them all. Red can release the hormone adrenaline, giving you a quick energy boost, which is helpful if feeling run-down or lacking in motivation. Being fit and healthy is all about balance, and exercise is vital to keeping our bodies moving, active and energised. Red is one of the best colours to wear to propel you to action, as it can raise your blood pressure and metabolism, even if it's just for short bursts of activity.

ORANGE is a combination of primary red and yellow, encapsulating the wonderfully warming and uplifting properties of both, making it a super happy colour. Orange speaks of happiness, adventure and optimism. Think about the softer shades of salmon, coral, apricot, tangerine, peach, and team with any of your neutrals if you feel it's too stimulating for your comfort zone.

YELLOW, another primary, is a strong reactive colour for your eyes, and is mentally stimulating and joyful, just as sunlight is to the earth. It really can get the creative juices going, but sometimes it's best in small doses if you are wearing it for long periods of time. There are many shades and tones of yellow to choose from dependant on your warm or cool undertones to make sure you glow in your best light, from lemon to mustard. Yellow can be balanced by adding cool blues and purples.

Your personal prescription of comfort colours

SPRING'S comfort zone:

Spring is a bright, warm palette. Highlighting the hotter end of the spectrum: reds, corals, yellows, so consider going softer into Spring's pastel shades if you want or need to tone things down:

- Red: bright, poppy, scarlet, pillar box, mango, bright red orange
- Yellow: bright, daffodil, clear golden
- Green: bright, lime, bright emerald, blue-green, aqua
- Blue: bright, turquoise, periwinkle, light navy, electric
- Pink: bright, hot, coral, salmon
- Orange: bright, mango, apricot, peach, coral
- Purple: bright purple, bright violet, lilac
- Brown: camel, warm stone, golden brown, tan
- Neutrals: bright navy, warm grey, cream, ivory, gold

Spring's comfort combinations:

- Lime green and pink: wonderfully harmonious, keeps the balance whilst being uplifting and compassionate, a loving, supportive combination

- Bright lilac and turquoise: a combination that helps in all mediation, is inspiring and meditative, whilst instilling a sense of calm with controlled communication
- Peach and cream: a softer version of orange, a shade that represents happiness, sociability and celebration, together with a fresh, open outlook
- Bright navy and red: a strong combination of great commitment, and loyalty together with a sense of excitement and enthusiasm for the future
- Golden yellow and tan: this is a really warm hug, full of the joys of Spring, but grounded and centred in a gentle stabilising way
- Camel/tan/cream/gold/warm grey/bright navy accessories

AUTUMN'S comfort zone:

Autumn is a very warm, muted and earthy palette. Highlighting the yellow/golden hotter end of the spectrum and instead of black you have many warm comforting brown shades to choose from, so consider light to dark variations of the following:

- Red: orange-red, rust, brick, bittersweet, warm tomato red
- Yellow: mustard, golden, tan, camel
- Green: khaki, olive, yellow-green, dark lime
- Blue: teal, marine, muted turquoise
- Pink: dark salmon, dark peach, muted pink
- Orange: burnt orange, dark apricot, coral, deep peach, terracotta
- Purple: muted purple
- Brown: coffee, bronze, camel, warm beige, caramel, chocolate
- Neutrals: all warm browns, warm grey, navy blue, cream

Autumn's comfort combinations:

- Teal blue and chocolate: comforting calming blue in its warmest shade along with rich, luxurious chocolate brown, just delightfully indulgent
- Burnt orange and khaki green: optimistic, uplifting orange enjoys a wonderful balance with muted warm khakis and olive greens
- Mustard yellow and warm grey: joyful, mentally stimulating and creative, this shade of yellow is happy to be grounded by practical and efficient grey
- Brick red and coffee: the confident, outgoing qualities of warm red feel comfortable and at home with the earthiness of coffee
- Dark lime and cream: green's balancing nature combined with cream will be a refreshing breath of clean air from this harmonious pairing
- Warm browns/bronze/antique gold/cream/warm grey and navy accessories

SUMMER'S comfort zone:

Summer is a light, cool and delicate colour palette. Highlighting the cooler end of the spectrum; blues, pinks and purples, so consider any shades of the following to feel comfortable and cool:

- Red: raspberry, watermelon, light burgundy
- Yellow: light lemon
- Green: mint, light emerald
- Blue: powder blue, light aqua, periwinkle, muted turquoise, cadet, muted navy, blue-grey, baby blue, pastel icy blue
- Pink: rose, carnation, pastel pink, powder pink, light muted pink, pale fuchsia

- Orange: muted soft peach
- Purple: muted purple, lavender, violet
- Brown: taupe, almond, rose beige
- Neutrals: navy blue, dove grey, silver-grey, mid-charcoal grey, blue-grey, pearl white

Summer's comfort combinations:

- Rose pink and violet: a heavenly mix of compassionate pink and creative inspiring violet, get crafting in these colours
- Periwinkle blue and dove grey: a calming quiet space for contemplation and putting good communication into a practical arena
- Mint green and almond: a refreshing, zingy zone of uplifting green and grounding almond brown but in a soft and light shade, nothing too heavy to bog you down
- Lavender and navy blue: an inspiring mix of dreamy, deep thinking purple and the one-to-one communicator that you are and darker blue will gift you
- Navy blue/dove grey/silver/rose gold/pearly white accessories

WINTER'S comfort zone:

Whilst Winter types can wear black better than all of the other seasons, don't be tempted into wearing all black all of the time. I appreciate it's a lovely way to keep private and be creative for hours on end, but it can also drain your energy too, if you wear it too much. You could consider one of your other 'neutrals' instead. Add one or two of your vibrant shades into the mix to keep you feeling upbeat as well as comfortable in any of the following cool shades:

- Red: blue red, true red, cool bright red, burgundy red,

maroon
- Pink: fuchsia, magenta, plum, hot cool pink, icy pastel pink
- Blue: bright cool turquoise, cobalt, electric, icy pastel blue, dark navy
- Green: pine, forest, emerald, dark jade, pastel green
- Purple: blue-violet, royal, ultraviolet, deep purple
- Yellow: acid, neon, icy pastel yellow
- Grey: charcoal, grey-black, silver-grey, icy pastel grey
- Black and brilliant white
- Neutrals: black, black-brown, navy blue, charcoal grey, taupe, white, pastel grey

Winter's comfort combinations:

- Fuchsia pink and charcoal grey: this a fun-loving, high spirited shade of pink, so really lifts your mood, and worn with grey gives it drama whilst also creates the space that you like to be in for ultimate comfortable living
- Ultraviolet and black: this is really a super charged creative zone for you, an inspired combination that will have you drawing, drafting, inventing, inspiring for hours
- Acid yellow and navy blue: this is a great combo for you, to feel that hit of joyfulness that yellow brings whilst keeping you cool and calm and collected
- Burgundy red and brilliant white: give yourself a confidence boost, whilst keeping a clear head to see the path ahead clearly and with a new fresh approach
- Black/charcoal/silver/platinum/white/navy blue accessories

Chapter 7

Welcome to Your Colourful Home

Diagnose the mood & emotion desired in your home
Prescribe yourself a colourful dose of optimism at home
Statement colour ideas to give your home a lift
Let your personality shine through your interiors
Spring – Autumn – Summer – Winter at home

I don't know about you but I love a TV home decorating show! It's such fun watching other people transform their inside worlds into havens of comfort and joy. I think it's fair to say that one person's idea of interior heaven can be another's hell. Purple bedrooms and lime bathrooms, retro, bright, neutral or bold, it's always fun to have a peep into how others live.

In recent years the common theme has been neutral shades of grey; from anything to do with elephants to slate, with a hint of mint thrown in along the way. However, these days things are shifting. It seems that the movement towards warmer, richer and more 'comforting' colours is starting to infiltrate the world of interiors.

So, I thought it would be fun to help you create your own colourful home in an optimistic way. By bringing your authentic personality through your already prescribed 'Happy Colours' into your living environment to give it the boost it needs now. The benefits of understanding your own personal colour scheme mean you can create a harmonious living environment for yourself and your family. Achieved simply and economically, avoiding the high cost of major renovations.

Many of you are deciding not to move house, but maybe need a change in décor to your current abodes. Now is the time to realise that with clever use of colour you could refresh and enhance your home, using colour to emotionally support you. Lift the roof, raise the floorboards and celebrate indoors.

With this simple, effective colour diagnostic system below you can choose the mood of each room you want to create, by looking at the psychological benefits of individual colours and how they could combine for home harmony. See how these colour preferences can be used in different rooms of the house so everyone gets to express their personality too.

Diagnose the mood & emotion desired in your home

- Think clearly about what the purpose is of each room and the space.
- Do you want a calming, relaxing environment in your living area, whilst your kitchen is full of fun?
- Do you have a study or children's playroom that could do with some mental stimulation to boost creativity?
- Do you want to add some romance to your bedroom without insomnia?
- Do you need to increase productivity in your study now you are working from home?
- Do you want each room to look warmer or cooler, bigger or smaller?

We are now going to look at how you can choose which colour or combinations to harness the positive power of colour elevating each room to highlight the mood and emotion desired.

Prescribe yourself a colourful dose of optimism in every room

A RED room:

RED benefits:
Energising – stimulating – dynamic – passionate – enthusiastic – reactive – vibrant

Why use RED:
Red is an instant mood booster – can raise the temperature in a room as it's the hottest colour on the rainbow spectrum – can make a large space appear smaller – red can instantly make you feel invigorated – is stimulating to all who sit in a red room – many shades to choose from cool pastel reds to dark, rich warmer reds – fast food restaurants often use red to encourage quick eating and a rapid turnaround on tables.

Eating areas:
Red stimulates the appetite and encourages great conversation – if painting your kitchen or dining room big bold blocks of red, expect high energy, but quick burnout – use red as ACCENTS in your pots and pans, crockery or ornaments – cabinets, curtains and paintings are a great way to add a burst of red.

Hallways:
Red is a welcoming colour so use it to invite your guests into your home – aside from red walls, consider a lovely red mat or rug to give yourself some red-carpet glamour!

Living areas:
Red is warming and comforting – use it in living areas if you want to increase conversation and add lots of energy – think red walls or soft furnishings, curtains, carpets, pictures, vases, or

throws – patterns and prints are a lovely way to incorporate red without going too bold.

Bedrooms:

BEWARE too much red in a sleeping area – YES to passion but NOT for good sleep – use sparingly please if you don't want insomnia to strike – candles, picture frames and maybe a red cushion or two or a lamp shade will be quite sufficient to get the balance right.

Top RED Tips:

- Always consider your shade of red and how much you use in a room
- The lighter colours are more uplifting, with the darker, heavier shades being more oppressive over time
- Decorate one wall for a vibrant hit of happiness, or a single rug to get into the red zone

A PINK room:

PINK benefits:

Nurturing – soothing – comforting – romantic

Why use PINK:

Gentler and softer than red – shades range from cool roses, to rich magenta and vibrant fuchsia to dusky zones with peachy, salmon pinks warming things up – pink is romantic and loving, a caring, protective colour – pink speaks of love.

Hallways:

Welcome in the world in dusky, peachy pinks, combined with fresh green plants or paintings, rugs or lamps, to ground pink's flighty nature.

Bedrooms:

Pink is love, and romance, and a comforting colour to sleep in, and children's bedrooms can really benefit from the cossetting protection of loving pink – think pink curtains, bedspreads; walls in pale shades with stronger blues is a beautiful and powerful combination – go stronger and more vibrant pink to really boost the mood of the room.

Top PINK tips:
- Hot pink and violet are great bedroom combinations for a teenage room
- Combining the qualities of creativity, independence and inner reflection along with support for change

An ORANGE room:

ORANGE benefits:

Happy – cheerful – optimistic – sociable – adventurous – stimulating – warming – comforting

Why use ORANGE:

It stimulates the senses, being a combination of energising, warming red and joyful, sunny yellow – it's a wonderful colour for socialising in your home – a big upside is its ability to make people feel optimistic and happy.

Eating areas:

Like red, orange is also a great colour to encourage lots of fabulous chat and is a great appetite stimulant too – if your kitchen or dining area is large or feels cold, shades of orange can warm it up and will make it feel smaller too – use this colour sparingly if you don't want your room to be overwhelmingly orange – pots, pans, glassware, pictures and plates can all add that hit of happiness orange brings – or a fruit bowl full of oranges, peaches, apricots and mandarins will instantly lift a table.

Living spaces:

Orange is full of radiance, and again encourages sociability, so if this is the main purpose of your living area, choose some orange to lift your spirits – there are many shades to choose from, including soft, delicate pastels in apricot and peach, or corals – but if you want something warmer, consider terracotta and burnt orange – blocks of richer orange can look fabulous, combined with blues to bring balance into a living space – consider bringing orange flowers into communal areas to give everyone you live with and yourself that hit of happiness from seeing orange's warming rays.

Hallways:

Welcome your guests with the warmth and friendliness that orange brings, the moment you open your front door – the softer, paler shades of peach used with white or cream will open up a small hallway, or use darker, deeper orange to create depth in a large entrance hall.

Top ORANGE tips:

- You only need a hint of orange to uplift the spirits, and make a bold and warming statement
- Dynamic in its brighter shades, or rich, earthy muted shades of terracotta, use with deep blues, and dark wood for a luxurious look, or light pine to lighten the mood

A YELLOW Room:

YELLOW benefits:

Joyful – mentally stimulating – optimistic – upbeat – sunny –

cheerful – individualistic – enlightening

Why use YELLOW:
It stimulates the mind to get creative – it literally brings the sunshine inside – is warming and welcoming particularly in golden shades – it really is a colour that can make people smile, however, it's also one that can make you run for cover if you visually overdose so consider how much yellow to use in any room.

Eating areas:
Warming yellows create an environment of happiness and sunshine, and will brighten up a kitchen or dining room – yellow is a wonderful colour for children to be surrounded in during daylight hours, because it's stimulating and mentally creative – consider decorating one or two walls yellow instead of an entire room so as not to go overboard – use lots of lights (yellow tinted) to experience the glow in these areas – a bowl of lemons will instantly lift any kitchen surface.

Studies/playrooms:
Yellow is one of the BEST colours to choose for these areas, due to its mentally creative qualities – wonderful for children's daytime play areas to get them motivated, active and creating things – at the end of the day, they could be exhausted and need to go into a blue room to sleep – for everyone working who needs to focus on getting their minds active put some yellow in a study or an office.

Bathrooms:
Imagine waking up and washing in a ray of sunshine, that's what having a yellow bathroom can do for you!

Bedrooms:

Use with CARE... particularly in children's bedrooms – yellow is so mentally stimulating it can keep the mind working and not create a relaxing environment to sleep in – use accents of yellow in cushions, lights, patterns in décor, to get that hit of happiness without causing insomnia!

Top YELLOW tips:

- If yellow isn't a colour you want to indulge in your home, consider a yellow-based CREAM, a soft version that incorporates yellow's joy-giving properties
- Also, have yellow flowers around you, then you can bring them in and out when you need yellow's hit of sunlight

A GREEN room:

GREEN benefits:

Peaceful – balancing – reassuring – friendly – refreshing – calming – strengthening

Why use GREEN:

Green sits midway on the colour wheel, so can be cooled down by adding some blue, or warmed up with yellow – due to its balancing properties and being so restful on the eyes, green is used in many institutions like hospitals to help keep people feeling cool and calm – bring nature inside with many shades of green to choose from, it's a delight to decorate with.

Living areas:

If the idea of a living space for you and your family is to chill out and feel calm then choose a shade of green that you love – if you want to use this space to entertain in then consider adding some red to feel energised and stimulated – in its paler shades it can make a small room look bigger, and create a sense of well-being too – communal areas can all be enhanced by bringing in some balancing green for equilibrium – painting kitchen chairs green is a lovely way to incorporate a shade you love, and team it with a tablecloth or cushions.

Studies:

Green is a fabulous colour to have in a study or home office – as the great 'decision maker' it's a wonderful colour to enable you to see all sides of a problem or situation plus you get to feel balanced when working, neither too stimulated nor too relaxed.

Hallways:

Green can be warmed up to create a welcoming and friendly hallway – use with white or cream to keep it looking fresh and clean.

Bedrooms:

Use the cooler shades of green for a restful and good night's sleep – anything that goes into the 'lime' warm category should be used in small doses, as the yellow mix will be stimulating – combine with pink to add some romance into your room in softer shades, or provide your family with some uplifting hot hits of nurturing pink.

Top GREEN tips:

- Use green plants in abundance in your home
- There is some research to suggest that they can increase productivity, and are great for stress busting as well as bringing the joy of nature inside

A BLUE room

BLUE benefits:
Tranquil – calming – conservative – peaceful – relaxing – serene

Why use BLUE:
Think of the sky and the sea and how relaxed you feel on holiday whilst surrounded by both – it helps to calm the nervous system – this is probably why blue is often voted the world's favourite colour – in our homes it can be used to positive effect, helping to create peaceful, restorative spaces.

Living areas:
If you choose to create an oasis of calm in your communal areas, then blue is for you – a fabulous colour for communicating in a trusting and diplomatic way, so use it for family rooms where you want to feel serene – choose your shades with care, the lighter ones will lift a small room – dark ones will make it smaller and in large amounts can sometimes be depressing – the trick is to consider one or two walls in a bold shade and maybe add some vibrant yellow to brighten things up, and have lots of lights to balance your blues.

Kitchens:
It's cool to use blue in kitchens nowadays, as a calming colour if you spend more time than usual cooking and in your family comfort zone – shades or accents of blue walls or cupboards combined with vibrant warming oranges and bright reds can liven things up – blue shelves are another option, or blue recipe books!

Bathrooms:
Blue is an obvious bathroom choice – as an individual space

of peace and relaxation, what better colour to feel completely rested in – bathe surrounded by blue 'sky' and light some candles to flicker some warming light, for a spa-like indulgence of the senses.

Bedrooms:

A perfect choice for a bedroom, to enable rest and a good night's sleep – blue can have a beneficial calming effect on your nervous system – so if you have had a stressful day, being surrounded by blue at night-time can help to recharge the batteries for you and your children too – be mindful of either a warm or a cool blue base and add in some compassionate pink, a lovely bedroom combo.

Top BLUE tips:

- Consider turquoise as a really uplifting shade of blue – it tends to have some green in the mix so you can benefit from the psychological and balancing properties of both
- Turquoise adds a playful element to any room, and looks dramatic alongside darker blue
- Using tonal blues can combine well with shades of warming, stimulating orange
- A blue ceiling is a wonderful way to bring the sky inside!

A PURPLE room:

PURPLE benefits:

Regal – luxurious – meditative – dreamy – creative – inspiring – visionary

Why use PURPLE:

There are many shades of purple, depending on how much blue or red is used, so you can warm it up or cool it down

– violet comprising both of these powerful colours is able to bring balance and strength – as the shortest wavelength of light, it is the most restful on our eyes, so a lovely colour to surround yourself in, for any form of meditation or calming of the mind.

Living areas:

I believe that accents of purple or violet in a living space can add sophistication and drama in small doses – so consider one deep purple wall, or cushions, curtain or sofa/chair fabrics with purple in a mix or even a purple lamp or pot – lilac walls can be an uplifting alternative to deep ultraviolet.

Bedrooms:

Violet and purple are a lovely calming alternative to using blue in a bedroom – also consider using the softer, pastel shades if lighting is a problem – for good sleep, they are helpful in times of change so for children growing up, can offer strength as well as rest – use in a bedroom with some clarifying, cleansing white.

Top PURPLE tips:

- If purple isn't your preferred choice in your home, you can always use accessories like tablecloths, napkins and candles for any form of special occasion
- Spice purple up with warming oranges and yellows
- It looks especially luxurious when used with metallics of gold and silver in tableware or lamps in any room

BROWN:

Brown is all about stability, grounding, and feeling centred – it is one of the best colours for creating a comforting and warming atmosphere in any room and for a rustic feel – use as a 'neutral' either in décor or wooden pine/oak floors or furniture

– choose delicate browns or go rich and dark depending on your taste and how much light you have in your room – consider the colour of your materials; brown or tan leather chairs and sheepskin throws, with velvet cushions.

GREY:

Grey has been in favour for years – whilst predominantly a cool colour being a black and white mix, you can warm it up by adding some yellow or combine with other cool colours like blue and purple to change it again – as a 'neutral' it's versatile, practical and gives a room a classic look – think 'dove' grey for sophistication, or dark stone floors or walls to add a modern, hi-tech feel to any room – grey works in harmony with other pastel colours, and more vibrant, hotter ones too – in fact, its versatility is possibly why it is so popular.

BLACK:

Black will of course make a room darker – as a colour it absorbs light – however, as an accent colour it can look super dramatic and will make any room look cool and modern – use in accessories in details like picture frames, marble fireplaces, lamp stands, coffee tables and in art and photographs too – these can add depth and interest to any room.

WHITE:

One of the main benefits of white is how it makes any living space bigger – white reflects light so it allows any other colours you choose to really shine – white is clean, fresh and timeless – there are also many white shades to choose from – keep it cool with blues, pinks and greys or warm it up with yellows and browns – magnolia, having been popular for years, is of course seen as a cream; white mixed with yellow, therefore an uplifting arena.

SILVER:

Cool – hi-tech – spacy – edgy – modern silver will add shine and gloss to any surface or detail, with picture frames, taps, kitchen appliances, cutlery, vases, lamps, etc.

GOLD:

Glamorous – warming – luxurious – sparkling – glittering gold – will add excitement and glitz to all rooms – brass or copper into pots and pans, coffee tables, lamp bases, doorknobs etc. to upgrade any look.

Expert Interior Decorators Sabrina Panizza & Aude Lerin's top tip on injecting colour into your home: "One of the most effective ways to inject colours into your home is experimenting with paint colours; although it is easy to reach for white, you can do so much more if you get to grips with bold, rich and timeless colours. Depending on how daring you are, you could opt for a feature wall, or use colours to enhance (or create) architectural charm. By highlighting the design and details in this way, you will add a strong dose of character, energy and vibrancy to your living space."

Statement colour ideas to give your HOME a LIFT:

Front doors: what better way to welcome people into your home than a colourful front door! Greet everyone, with a big joyful yellow hello or go-green offering a friendly entrance, with an environment of inner calm.

Ceilings: bring the sky in and paint a ceiling in a joyful shade of blue, particularly uplifting aqua; bold or striped; think pink in a bedroom, and drift off to sleep in a cossetting, comfort zone of love.

Hanging lamps: instantly brighten up a room with a statement colour light shade – simple, super impactful whilst adding a dash of colour in a cost-effective way.

Flooring: get some colour onto the floor for happy feet in tiles or floorboards; checks, or retro patterns; in blues, greens or yellows to instantly freshen up a tired-looking room.

Shelves: paint shelves or find a cabinet with shelves built in, and choose a colour to make you happy, and display pots, crockery or books in bold colours to lift up a neutral shelf.

Baskets: add some colour to a room with a wicker basket for laundry in a bathroom, or waste bin in bedrooms or living areas.

Luxe accessories: blankets, throws, bedspreads, cushions; in velvet, velour, silks and satins; bright colours, as well as warm rich comforting colours and glorious prints and florals.

Crystals: come in many different colours and sizes to suit your needs – rose quartz is a beautiful pink stone that works well in a bedroom, encouraging pleasant dreams – purple amethyst is perfect for meditating and placed by your computer to absorb negative waves – clear quartz can be used in any living area to zing in some positive energy – make sure you cleanse a new crystal in warm salted water and leave it in direct sunlight to dry for as long as possible – you need it to be full of fresh sparkling energy to benefit your home.

Celebrity Interior Designer Anna Standish's top tip on making neutrals colourful: "When introducing a client to the multiple powers of interior design, colour is a key element. Not being able to see past grey or taupe is a common complaint, so I take the neutral tone as far to the right or the left (on the colour spectrum) as I can. Grey can move sideways into the grey-blue tones, maybe reaching duck-egg blue, and taupe could be gently moved into taupe-green tones, to reach sage green. Balance is also key, so look for a bold two-colour mix, with a third contrasting colour to add an unexpected twist and ensure a scheme never looks over coordinated, or predictable in following trends."

Let your personality SHINE through your interiors

- Your home is an extension of your personality and an environment of self-expression, with every room having a purpose.
- Colour schemes in interiors can help to create a healthy balance for your well-being by tapping into your own personal colour palette.
- By analysing your individual colours and having taken an in-depth look at your personality, you will have determined which of the seasonal categories you belong to, whether it's the warm Spring or Autumn, or the cool Summer or Winter.
- These colour palettes can be used to positively benefit your moods, as well as enhancing your living spaces to create happy places for yourself and your family to relax in, play in and have wonderful experiences in.
- If you are a lively, sociable Spring type you will need to be surrounded in bright, warm shades to feel really happy and at ease in your own home. Dynamic, driven Autumn's best colours will be gorgeously golden and full of rich, earthy tones.
- Perhaps you are more of the diplomatic, creative Summer who loves cool pastels, or the Winter perfectionist, who favours a neon accent colour with black and white. Let's now take a look at your personality at home and suggest some fun ways you can consider adding in a colourful dose of optimism with your best colours.

SPRING at home

- Your Spring home will be light, bright and often full of vibrant colour schemes.
- Consider your furniture preferences in light types of

coloured wood, yellow based like pine or bamboo.
- Fabrics in bright warm colours are your favourite, because really dark colour schemes can bring your mood down. Ensure you always have a balance in light and dark shades to keep you feeling upbeat and balanced.
- Consider colourful florals and patterns, as well as bold designs in your fabrics and décor.
- Favourite decorating colours for you are the sunny yellows, brighter blues, aqua greens and peaches along with coral. Warm pinks and creams are also popular.
- Your neutral shades are cream, magnolia, honey beige, camel, green-grey and bright navy.

AUTUMN at home

- Your Autumn home will be full of rich warm browns.
- You love brick and stone in earthy, muted tones.
- It's important for you to be surrounded in warm colours that make you feel comforted.
- Fabrics that are patterned with tribal influences, geometric prints and particularly animal print will be favourable to you.
- Dark antique furniture appeals to you.
- Terracotta is a wonderful colour to lift your mood, along with all shades of orange, warm brick red and the many warm golden and deep rich browns, olive and khaki greens combine beautifully with bronze and gold too.
- These colours can be offset with your neutral warm tones of brown, stone, beige and camel with cream.

SUMMER at home

- Your Summer home will be full of soft, delicate colours in your fabrics and furnishings.

- Subtle prints in pastel shades and florals will give you the sense of calm and order that makes you feel happy and at ease.
- You will like to decorate in colours that are cooling to your senses and that harmonise beautifully with each other.
- Favourite decorating colours for you are pastels in all cool colours. Particularly blues, like cornflower and sky, the rose pinks and lavender purples.
- These combine aesthetically well with your neutral cool greys, almond taupe and pearl white.

WINTER at home

- Your Winter home will be full of dramatic bold, solid colours, and you love to use black, white and grey along with accents of colour.
- For this reason, you will favour silver, chrome and metal in your neutrals and metallics.
- Think about black or grey sofas and chairs, with white walls and splashes of vibrant coloured artwork in neon pinks, yellows and reds or change up the mix to suit you.
- Your cool Winter colours (aside from black and white) include fuchsia and magenta pink, ultraviolet, electric blue and forest green.
- Combine colours with your neutrals black and white, charcoal grey, silver and navy blue.
- You have a dramatic palette, so just two colours in a room will often make you happiest.

Chapter 8

Colour yourself positive

Having completed this book, I hope you will feel a sense of joy and excitement, knowing what your personal, positive rainbow colours are. The art of using them can prove to be a great aid to boosting your mood, looking good and expressing your personality through your wardrobe and in your home. Nurturing yourself, caring for your inner needs through harnessing the benefits that colour offers you, can be very empowering and a true gift to yourself.

Whether you feel that bright red is the colour that makes you feel confident, gets you complimented and makes you smile. Or that you attribute these positive qualities to a cool shade of turquoise, I hope that discovering your happiest colours to wear or put into your home helps you feel more centred and balanced in our ever-changing and challenging world.

It's been a pleasure to have you along with me on this colourful journey. I sincerely hope that whatever your age or stage in life, you delight in prescribing yourself *A Colourful Dose of Optimism* to enhance every area of your lifestyle. I have endeavoured to share with you my interpretation of colour in all its amazing glory and its positive powers. However, I believe it's important to always keep an open mind as to how much of anything is right for each of us as individuals at any given time. Colour is a wonderfully subjective arena of life, and is there for the taking, in whichever way you wish.

Enjoy choosing your happy colours, those that make you sparkle and shine, and may therapeutically work for you at any given time, for ultimate well-being, now and forever!

With colourful love

Jules

References & contacts

The author

Jules Standish is "The Colour Counsellor" – an image consultant specialising in colour

Author of *How Not to Wear Black* and *The Essential Guide to Mindful Dressing*

Head of Colour at the London College of Style

Professional Colour Consultant, tutor, speaker, presenter

Colour expert for national newspapers and the media

www.colourconsultancy.co.uk

www.hownottowearblack.co.uk

@julesstandishcolour @hownottowearblack

jules@colourconsultancy.co.uk

Foreword

Wendy Elsmore Fashion & Style Expert – Director London College of Style

LCS is a global leader in creative industry immersed training London-based training and interactive online courses in fashion, personal styling, colour analysis, interior design, make-up, blogging, photography, nutrition

Please contact for all training: www.londoncollegeofstyle. com @londoncollegeofstyle

Endorsements

Annie Hughes Counsellor

anniehughescounselling@gmail.com

Karen Oppegard

Interior Consultant, Oppegard Designs

www.oppegard-designs.com

Sian Clarke Personal Stylist/LCS colour tutor

www.styledbysian.co.uk @styled_by_sian

hello@styledbysian.co.uk

Susie Webb Singer/Songwriter

https://www.youtube.com/watch?v=QLdJBpX9QJo

www.susiewebb.co.uk www.bossarocks.co.uk

Xan Phillips Broadcaster and Creative Director

xanphillips@gmail.com

Research References

Nieuwenhuis, Marlon & Knight, Craig & Postmes, Tom & Haslam, S. (2014) The Relative Benefits of Green Versus Lean Office Space: Three Field Experiments. *Journal of Experimental Psychology Applied* 20, doi:10.1037/xap0000024.

Hill, RA & Barton, RA (2005) Red enhances human performance in contests. *Nature* 435(7040): 293.

Wiedemann, D., Burt, DM, Hill, RA, & Barton, RA (2015) Red clothing increases perceived dominance, aggression and anger. *Biology Letters* 20150166.

Stephen Westland – Professor of Colour Science and Technology University of Leeds. https://ahc.leeds.ac.uk/design/staff/516/prof-stephen-westland

Opposites attract: Impact of background color on effectiveness of emotional charity appeals. https://www.sciencedirect.com/science/article/abs/pii/S0167811620300082?via%3Dihub#!

Smiling: https://www.sclhealth.org/blog/2019/06/the-real-health-benefits-of-smiling-and-laughing/

Personal Stylists & Fashion Experts (alphabetically)

Abbey Booth Personal Stylist based in Hertfordshire
Styling – advanced colour – wardrobe edits – LCS lecturer – radio presenter
@storieswithclothes
www.facebook.com/storieswithclothes

Angela Hathway Personal Stylist based in Amsterdam
Styling – shopping – advanced colour – online preloved

fashion store
@fashionandrepeat
@styling_by_angela
www.fashionandrepeat.com

Ania Bortnowska Personal Stylist based in London
Styling – wardrobe edits – advanced colour – shopping
@styled_by_ania
styledbyania@gmail.com

Aoife Duncan Personal Stylist based in Dublin, Ireland
Styling – image consultant – advanced colour – speaker – wardrobe edits – shopping – virtual style
@thestylebob
style@thestylebob.com
www.thestylebob.com

Charlotte Broadbent Personal Stylist based in London
Styling – TV presenter – speaker – impact coach – LCS lecturer – blogger – colour – fashion editor
@_charlotteloves_
www.charlotteloves.co.uk

Clare Watkins Personal Stylist based in Manchester
Styling – wardrobe edits – colour – LCS lecturer – virtual styling – shopping
@clarewatkins_stylist
www.clarewatkins.com
www.facebook.com/StylingbyClare/
https://twitter.com/stylist_clare

Daniel Shalom Assistant Buyer at Kurt Geiger
@_shalomshalom_
danielshalom@hotmail.co.uk

Elaine Davies Personal Stylist based in Edinburgh, Scotland
Styling – advanced colour – shopping – wardrobe edits
@stylish_touch_personal_stylist
elaine@stylishtouch.co.uk
www.stylishtouch.co.uk

Fleur McCrone Personal Stylist based in Sevenoaks, Kent
Celebrity styling – TV presenter QVC – LCS lecturer –
wardrobe edits – shopping – colour – virtual style
@stylistfleur
fleur@finestyling.co.uk
www.finestyling.co.uk

Jacqueline Lythe Personal Stylist based in London
Styling – wardrobe edits – shopping – advanced colour –
event style
@styled_by_jacqueline
www.styledbyjacqueline.co.uk

Janine Coney Style Coach based in Milton Keynes
Women's style coach – wardrobe edits – advanced colour –
shopping – image branding – online masterclasses – events
& workshops
@ownyourstyleuk
www.ownyourstyleuk.co.uk

Karina Morin "Third Eyed Babe" Image Consultant based in
Vancouver, Canada
Styling – holistic style coach
@thirdeyebabe.style

Kelly Hitchen Personal Stylist
Styling – advanced colour – health & beauty – founder of
#mycolourmedicine
@kelly_mystyle
kellyjh@gmail.com

Laura Cruickshank Personal Stylist based in Northants
Styling – advanced colour – co-host of #colourcrazyme
@ljcstyling

Laura Tippett-Wilson Personal Stylist based in York
Styling – blogger – plus size – advanced colour
@styledby_laura l
auraemilytw@hotmail.co.uk

Liv Styler Personal Stylist based in Surrey

Styling – advanced colour – wardrobe edits – personal shopping – online style
@liv_styler_
www.livStyler.co.uk

Lynn Deards Image Consultant based in High Wycombe
Styling – advanced colour – wardrobe edits – shopping
Founder
#notsavingitforbest
@lynnlovesshopping
www.styledbylynn.co.uk

Millie Coates Personal Stylist based in Tunbridge Wells, Kent
Styling – advanced colour – wardrobe edits – shopping – style parties
@_thestylephoenix_
millie@thestylephoenix.co.uk
www.thestylephoenix.co.uk

Monica Huaza Master Barre Trainer, Yoga Instructor & Personal Stylist
CEO "The Monica Method LLC" based in Boston, USA
@glamorousyogi
www.themonicamethod.com

Nancy Stevens Personal Stylist based in Milton Keynes
Styling – vlogger Podcaster and host of *The Nancy Stevens Show*
@_nancymk_
http://www.youtube.com/c/NancyStevens

Nick Hems Personal Stylist Menswear based in Bath
Styling – personal branding – advanced colour – shopping – online style
@iamnickhems
www.nickhemsstyle.co.uk

Nina Victoria Personal Stylist based in Surrey
Styling – advanced colour – wardrobe detox – shopping – virtual style

@_ninavictoria_
www.ninavictoria.co.uk

Peter Kane Personal Stylist based in Sheffield, Yorks
Styling – "Mr Colour" – wardrobe edits – designer – virtual
styling – LCS colour tutor – wardrobe declutter & restyle
@pjthepersonalstylist

Phill Tarling Celebrity Fashion Stylist based in London
Styling – image consultant – senior mentor FAD
@philltarling
www.philltarling.com

Saasha Scaife Personal Stylist based in Sydney, Australia
Styling – advanced colour – wardrobe edits – shopping
@styled_by_saasha
www.styledbysaasha.com

Sarah Cannon Personal Stylist based in Essex
Styling – wardrobe edits – advanced colour – e-styling –
shopping
@styleyounew
www.styleyounew.com

Sarah Thomson Personal Stylist based in Edinburgh, Scotland
Styling – advanced colour – wardrobe edits – shopping –
speaker
@sarahthomsonstyle
me@sarahthomsonstyle.com
www.sarahthomsonstyle.com

Shanna Elizabeth Personal Stylist based in London
Styling – wardrobe edits – shopping – advanced colour –
workshops
@shannaelizabethstylist
style@shannaelizabethstylist.com

Sian Clarke Personal Stylist based in London
Styling – advanced colour – LCS colour tutor – wardrobe
edits & restyle – shopping – virtual services
www.styledbysian.co.uk

@styled_by_sian

hello@styledbysian.co.uk

Tanya McMillan Personal Stylist based in Edinburgh, Scotland
Styling – wardrobe edits – advanced colour – shopping – events

@tanyasukistyle

www.tanyasukistyle.com

Terri Cooper Personal Stylist based in Dublin, Ireland
Styling – advanced colour – wardrobe edits – shopping – creative branding

@thestylecoop

#myfeelgoodfashion

info@thestylecoop.ie

Tracy Hooper Image Consultant based in Berkshire
Personal styling – professional colour consultant – LCS senior colour tutor – wardrobe edits – shopping – corporate training – virtual styling

@tracyjaynehooper

www.tracyjaynehooper.com

uk.linkedin.com/in/tracyjaynehooper

Vicky Wood Personal Stylist based in Berkshire
Styling – professional colour consultant – shopping – wardrobe edits

@vickywoodstyle

www.vickywoodstyle.com

Fashion, Jewellery & Accessory Brands and Boutiques

Benny Wilmot Cofounder of Frangipani "Shirts to live in"
Stunning colourful shirts for men
Online shop www.frangipani-style.com

@frangipanistyle

Camilla Ridley Founder and Designer of Ridley, the innovative London-based label that's individually made to flatter –

choose any style in any print and get it tailored to fit – retail shop and online

www.ridleylondon.com

@ridleylondon

Jo Edwards Founder of Jo Edwards Scarves London based in Sussex

Flaunt your outfit with a fabulous colourful scarf

Online scarf & accessory shop

www.joedwardslondon.com

@joedwardsscarves

Julia Watson Founder of TRIBE + FABLE based in Chelsea, London

Fashion, jewellery & interiors brand, with hand screen printing that creates inspiring combinations, ethically made on natural fabrics, semi-precious stones and colourful handmade semi-precious tassel necklaces

Online

www.tribeandfable.com

@tribeandfable

julia@tribeandfable.com

Liz Trendle Owner of award nominated "The Gate Boutique" Guildford, Surrey

Retail shop and online

www.thegateboutique.co.uk

@thegateboutiqueguildford

Melissa Nicholson Founder of Kettlewell Colours online fashion brand

Colourful wardrobe essentials in 300 colours – colour coded to each seasonal palette

Online shop

www.kettlewellcolours.co.uk

@kettlewellcolours

sales@kettlewellcolours.co.uk

Rachel Allpress Founder and owner of Fashion brand "Stoned

& Waisted" based in Suffolk

Luxury Shearling, knitwear and accessories

Online

www.stonedandwaistedfashion.com

@stonedwaisted

Tarra Rosenbaum Founder of Tarra Rosenbaum Jewellery Ltd based in London

Sells worldwide online and at her Altelier in London – beautifully handmade jewellery using colourful stones and vitreous enamel "Amulets that tell your talismanic story".

www.tarrarosenbaum.com

@tarrarosenbaum

tarra.rosenbaum@gmail.com

Interior Designers & Decorators

Anna Standish Interior Designer – BA Hons – Interior Architecture

On **the List** at House & Garden Magazine and an annually award-winning member of **Houzz Pro**

@annastandish.interiors

interiors@annastandish.com

www.annastandish.com

Sabrina Panizza & Aude Lerin Founders of pl_studio_uk – Interior Decorators based in London

Image Consultants – colour – interiors – style – art

@sabrina.panizza

@aude_lerin

@pl_studio_uk

@pl-studio.co.uk

SPIRITUALITY

O is a symbol of the world, of oneness and unity; this eye represents knowledge and insight. We publish titles on general spirituality and living a spiritual life. We aim to inform and help you on your own journey in this life.
If you have enjoyed this book, why not tell other readers by posting a review on your preferred book site?

Recent bestsellers from O-Books are:

Heart of Tantric Sex
Diana Richardson
Revealing Eastern secrets of deep love and intimacy to Western
couples.
Paperback: 978-1-90381-637-0 ebook: 978-1-84694-637-0

Crystal Prescriptions
The A-Z guide to over 1,200 symptoms and their healing crystals
Judy Hall
The first in the popular series of eight books, this handy little
guide is packed as tight as a pill-bottle with crystal remedies for
ailments.
Paperback: 978-1-90504-740-6 ebook: 978-1-84694-629-5

Take Me To Truth
Undoing the Ego
Nouk Sanchez, Tomas Vieira
The best-selling step-by-step book on shedding the Ego, using the
teachings of *A Course In Miracles*.
Paperback: 978-1-84694-050-7 ebook: 978-1-84694-654-7

The 7 Myths about Love...Actually!
The Journey from your HEAD to the HEART of your SOUL
Mike George
Smashes all the myths about LOVE.
Paperback: 978-1-84694-288-4 ebook: 978-1-84694-682-0

The Holy Spirit's Interpretation of the New Testament
A Course in Understanding and Acceptance
Regina Dawn Akers
Following on from the strength of *A Course In Miracles*, NTI
teaches us how to experience the love and oneness of God.
Paperback: 978-1-84694-085-9 ebook: 978-1-78099-083-5

The Message of A Course In Miracles
A translation of the Text in plain language
Elizabeth A. Cronkhite
A translation of *A Course in Miracles* into plain, everyday
language for anyone seeking inner peace. The companion
volume, *Practicing A Course In Miracles*, offers practical lessons
and mentoring.
Paperback: 978-1-84694-319-5 ebook: 978-1-84694-642-4

Your Simple Path
Find Happiness in every step
Ian Tucker
A guide to helping us reconnect with what is really important in
our lives.
Paperback: 978-1-78279-349-6 ebook: 978-1-78279-348-9

365 Days of Wisdom
Daily Messages To Inspire You Through The Year
Dadi Janki
Daily messages which cool the mind, warm the heart and guide
you along your journey.
Paperback: 978-1-84694-863-3 ebook: 978-1-84694-864-0

Body of Wisdom
Women's Spiritual Power and How it Serves
Hilary Hart
Bringing together the dreams and experiences of women across
the world with today's most visionary spiritual teachers.
Paperback: 978-1-78099-696-7 ebook: 978-1-78099-695-0

Dying to Be Free
From Enforced Secrecy to Near Death to True Transformation
Hannah Robinson
After an unexpected accident and near-death experience, Hannah
Robinson found herself radically transforming her life, while a
remarkable new insight altered her relationship with her father, a
practising Catholic priest.
Paperback: 978-1-78535-254-6 ebook: 978-1-78535-255-3

The Ecology of the Soul
A Manual of Peace, Power and Personal Growth for Real People
in the Real World
Aidan Walker
Balance your own inner Ecology of the Soul to regain your
natural state of peace, power and wellbeing.
Paperback: 978-1-78279-850-7 ebook: 978-1-78279-849-1

Not I, Not other than I
The Life and Teachings of Russel Williams
Steve Taylor, Russel Williams
The miraculous life and inspiring teachings of one of the World's
greatest living Sages.
Paperback: 978-1-78279-729-6 ebook: 978-1-78279-728-9

On the Other Side of Love
A woman's unconventional journey towards wisdom
Muriel Maufroy
When life has lost all meaning, what do you do?
Paperback: 978-1-78535-281-2 ebook: 978-1-78535-282-9

Practicing A Course In Miracles
A translation of the Workbook in plain language, with
mentor's notes
Elizabeth A. Cronkhite
The practical second and third volumes of The Plain-Language
A Course In Miracles.
Paperback: 978-1-84694-403-1 ebook: 978-1-78099-072-9

Quantum Bliss
The Quantum Mechanics of Happiness, Abundance, and Health
George S. Mentz
Quantum Bliss is the breakthrough summary of success and
spirituality secrets that customers have been waiting for.
Paperback: 978-1-78535-203-4 ebook: 978-1-78535-204-1

The Upside Down Mountain
Mags MacKean
A must-read for anyone weary of chasing success and happiness
– one woman's inspirational journey swapping the uphill slog for
the downhill slope.
Paperback: 978-1-78535-171-6 ebook: 978-1-78535-172-3

Your Personal Tuning Fork
The Endocrine System
Deborah Bates
Discover your body's health secret, the endocrine system, and
'twang' your way to sustainable health!
Paperback: 978-1-84694-503-8 ebook: 978-1-78099-697-4

Readers of ebooks can buy or view any of these bestsellers by clicking on the live link in the title. Most titles are published in paperback and as an ebook. Paperbacks are available in traditional bookshops. Both print and ebook formats are available online.

Find more titles and sign up to our readers' newsletter at http://www.johnhuntpublishing.com/mind-body-spirit

Follow us on Facebook at https://www.facebook.com/OBooks/ and Twitter at https://twitter.com/obooks